WORKING WITH L

The author comes from a family steeped in L.N.W.R. railway history. His grandfather started work at Crewe in 1866, and took part in the Anglo-Scottish races of 1895 as a top-link driver, retiring in 1922 as footplate inspector for the Crewe-Carlisle line. His father was shedmaster at Stafford from 1919 and later at the ex-L.N.W.R. shed at Swansea, where the author himself started as an apprentice fitter in 1932 – after failing the railway clerical examination, much to the disgust of his parents!

His story is well told, sounding a clear ring of authenticity as he describes the many problems confronting steam engine fitters who were saddled with maintaining the L.N.W. type locomotives at Swansea. Later he went to Bescot and afterwards, as relief fitter in the Salop district, performed holiday relief duties at sheds in Abergavenny and Tredegar. In 1941 he transferred to the ex-L.&Y. shed at Bolton, and went to Leighton Buzzard as fitter-in-charge before moving back to Swansea shed in 1946 as mechanical foreman.

He later returned to L.&Y. territory once more, as Chief Mechanical Foreman at Newton Heath, where he became Locomotive Shedmaster in 1960.

WORKING WITH LMS STEAM

H.C.H. BURGESS

BRADFORD BARTON

ISBN 0 85153 450 3

Produced by Lovell Baines Print Ltd

for the publishers

D. BRADFORD BARTON LTD

Trethellan House · Truro · Cornwall

CONTENTS

Two of our v.c.r. regulars – Nos. 7481 and 7480 at Clydach-on-Tawe with push-and-pull trains in August 1948. 7480 is pulling to Brynamman and 7481 is pushing her two-coach set to Swansea St. Thomas. *(Photo: H.C. Casserley)*

Looking north up the Tawe valley from the ex-M.R. station at Swansea (St. Thomas). From the sidings to the left a single line ran beside the river into the King's Dock, whilst access to the Prince of Wales Docks was from sidings to the right of the station. *(Photo: H.C. Casserley)*

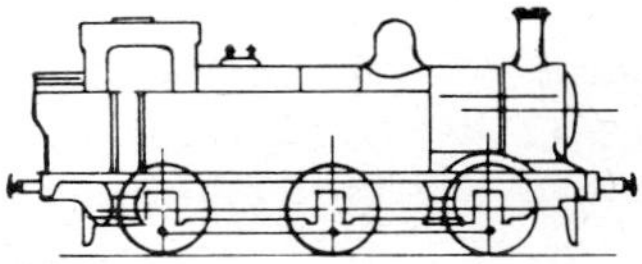

CHAPTER I

Day One

Many people contrive to retain mental images of important events in their lives, and this is certainly true of my first day at work as an apprentice fitter – an occasion I still recall vividly. The day was a Monday in March 1932 and the place was the now demolished ex-L.N.W.R. engine shed at the bottom of Paxton Street in Swansea. It was, even then, a rather decrepit building with a leaky roof, very prone to catch fire from the chimney sparks of locos standing beneath it, should any fireman be over zealous in the use of the blower.

The shed, which stood open to the west, had under its roof six pit roads, each with a pit outside for the use of enginemen during preparation. At the north side of the shed were the water tank, coal stage and ash pit roads, two storage sidings and the turntable road. The sands of Swansea Bay were only some fifty yards to the south, but a small marshalling yard, aptly named "Beach Sidings", lay between the shed and the sea wall. The entire area was a man-made promontory jutting into the sea, so that at high tide waves lapped its edge. But when the fierce sou-westerlies blew in winter, driving great breakers against the stout wall to send sheets of spray whistling across the shed, if one happened to be working on engines on the outside pits it was possible to taste the salt drying on one's lips.

This particular Monday was one such day, cold and blustery with squalls sweeping rain and spray several yards into the shed, almost reaching the wheel drop pit half way down No. 3 road. There 2317 stood in steam, waiting to have a broken pony spring renewed before working the 12/30 passenger train to Shrewsbury. At 7.45 that morning leading fitter Harry Kay had assigned me to the care of fitter Reginald David John Jenkins, who had been given the task of changing the spring on 2317 – one of Sir Henry Fowler's 2-6-4 tank engines, arguably the best of all his designs. In those days they were still fitted with separate brake gear operating on the bogie wheels, and braking was achieved from steam brake cylinders with opposing pistons mounted horizontally between the bogie wheels. Of necessity, steam connections to these cylinders were flexible pipes which carried the full boiler pressure of 200 p.s.i., and were prone to sudden failure by their very nature. Brake block life was painfully short, for they had a distressing tendency to "flange" and wear unevenly, and this combination of mechanical perverseness proved to be its Achilles heel – a couple of years later it was removed both from the 2-6-4 tanks and the Royal Scots, which had had the same brake gear fitted to their leading bogies.

One recalls another device of quite remarkable ingenuity fitted to the 2-6-4 tanks as originally built – the cylinder by-pass valves. A pipe of some 4″ or 5″ diameter was connected to special ports at both ends of the cylinder and ran inside the main frames; in the middle of this pipe was a valve, held in the closed position by steam as soon as the regulator was opened. With the regulator closed, the valve fell away from its seating, and the piston could now force the air entrapped at one end of the cylinder through the pipe to the opposite end of the cylinder, a feature which resulted in a very free – running locomotive, even with completely closed regulator. However, the valve was subject to some "chatter" when running with steam off and cases of failure began to occur with increasing frequency. Of course, a defective by-pass valve meant a total locomotive failure, since steam would now be admitted to both sides of the affected piston. We had to examine these valves every 5,000 miles and the method was to remove the bottom flange (held in position by six ½″ Whitworth bolts) which then exposed the brass actuating piston to view. It was secured to the valve by means of a threaded spindle and a brass nut, castellated to receive a copper cotter. If the nut and cotter were secure, in lieu of any instructions to the contrary, we would consider the valve satisfactory to run a further 5,000 miles. In view of the detailed maintenance instructions issued by present day B.R. Chief Mechanical Engineers, covering even the smallest item of equipment, one recalls with astonishment the almost complete lack of any such aid to maintenance staff during the days of steam traction, especially in the pre-war era. I feel sure that adequate maintenance instructions in respect of cylinder by-pass valves would have demanded removal of the entire assembly from the locomotive, followed by a complete strip-down on the bench. Obviously, the man-hours involved would have increased enormously and perhaps it was for this reason detailed instructions were never issued; whatever the reason, our inadequate examination procedure persisted at Swansea, failures rose to an unsupportable level and eventually the by-pass valves were removed.

Lest it be assumed that only Swansea fitters used this rather cursory method, one must add it was the norm everywhere – not only on this type but also on certain other types of locomotives so fitted – they all suffered the same fate.

After the by-pass valves were removed, drivers complained bitterly for many months about the resultant sluggishness of the "Crab" tanks – the name by which the 2-6-4 locos were known over the Central Wales line.

But I have digressed; back to 2317 and her broken spring – with the pony wheels on the wheel drop the work would probably take about an hour, less than half the time needed to lift the front end of the loco with hydraulic jacks. It was not until much later one came to realise how fortunate we were to have had the use of the wheel drop that day, since normally it was constantly employed dealing with hot axles, a recurrent malaise which afflicted many L.M.S. types and, for unique reasons, one that was endemic at Swansea.

I stood at the end of the shed to watch 2317 haul the six coach 12/30pm Shrewsbury train over the viaduct from Victoria station that day and saw the train out of sight as it headed west round Swansea Bay. Victoria station stood at street level about a mile east of the loco shed. Immediately upon leaving the station, trains were faced by a quarter mile of 1 in 40 gradient, which lifted the tracks up to a viaduct spanning an entrance to the South Dock and several streets. Opposite the shed the line began a gradual descent, returning to sea level by the time it reached Swansea Bay station, two miles from Victoria. This level was maintained a further two miles before an approach gradient lifted the tracks on to a bridge over the Mumbles road, through Mumbles Road station and inland up a 1 in 70 climb into the beautiful, thickly wooded Clyne Valley.

It was the two-mile stretch between Swansea Bay and Mumbles Road stations which provided the unique environment so conducive to hot bearings and excessive wear in other moving parts. Nowhere in the British Isles has a length of track been regarded with such grateful reverence by loco maintenance staff as was this one. It was our benefactor, providing not inconsiderable amounts of overtime and work for at least one more fitter than would have normally been required. Between these two stations the tracks were laid over sand dunes – sleepers and ballast there must have been yet nobody but the platelayers ever saw them, for they were buried in soft, fine sand which rose in all-pervading clouds to find its way into bearing surfaces each time a train passed over.

When the winter sou-westerlies blew, from the District Traffic Manager's viewpoint matters got even worse; from where we stood it was manna from heaven. . . . The section became totally blocked by deep drifts of sand, and emergency ballast trains were called out, with scores of platelayers to shovel sand into wagons, and on these occasions an air of *joie de vivre* would permeate the fitting staff. Even if working in that horror of horrors, a smokebox, they would laugh cheerily and wave joyously to each other, thinking about all the overtime to come. Meanwhile, a mile down the road in the Traffic Manager's office at Victoria station, gloom would hang like a black cloud as north-bound traffic was diverted over G.W. metals, and the figures of lost revenue were worked out.

The gales of the winter 1932–33 were particularly severe and quite unusual in their frequency, finally provoking the L.M.S. into preventive action. Word began to spread among us that the Civil Engineer intended to replace the existing lineside fences with ones specially designed to exclude blown sand; they were going to be ten feet tall, the local permanent way ganger told us, with a mischievous grin on his face. Normally a nice man well-liked by all of us, on this occasion his attitude as he imparted this dread news put us all off him – never again would we regard him as a friend. . . .

During the next month or two we kept ourselves *au fait* with the progress of the new fence, whilst the junior hand fitter, who would be first to get the chop should it succeed in its purpose, cast about for a new job. The nearest he came to one was the offer of temporary work on the Prince of Wales dock, unloading pit props on timber boats out of the St. Lawrence River. Fortunately, it never came to that – the new fence erected along the two-mile windward side of the line was a paltry affair which proved totally ineffective and the problem of drifting sand remained unsolved right up to the time the line was closed.

My parents were Crewe people, and after serving an apprenticeship at Crewe North shed and working there as a fitter, my father was appointed shed foreman at Stafford in 1919; it was not until after Nationalisation that the more resounding nomenclature "Locomotive Shedmaster" was adopted from the L.N.E.R. for these positions. Of course, I went to the shed with my father on every possible occasion – usually on Sunday mornings, when the place was full of Princes, Georges, Cauliflowers, Coal Tanks, and 0-8-0 freight engines. The North Staffordshire Railway also kept a loco here and worked trains into the Potteries from a bay platform on the up side at the north end of the station. I heard men referring to this railway as the "Knotty" but it wasn't until I saw the Staffordshire knot emblem on the coaching stock I realised why. Even in post electrification days, one heard Longsight men referring to London trains via Stoke-on-Trent as working over the "Knotty".

The Great Northern Railway also managed to achieve a somewhat tenuous toehold in Stafford, and had running powers over the L.N.W.R. for some two hundred yards north of the station, at which point its track branched east through Weston, Chartley and Grindley to a point near Bramshall, where they joined the North Staffordshire Railway with running powers via Uttoxeter, Sudbury and Tutbury to Great Marston. At this place the Great Northern's own tracks branched south to Burton and north via Etwall and Mickleover to Derby, where a splendid iron bridge, nowadays beautifully preserved by the authorities, carried the tracks over Friar Gate towards Nottingham.

After the amalgamation, when the North Staffs locos had lost their identity among the drab black of the L.M.S., the occasional green L.N.E. engine stood out like a beacon at Stafford.

In those days Stafford loco shed comprised two four-road wooden-roofed buildings between which ran the turntable, coal-stage and ashpit roads. The offices, messrooms, stores and fitting shop adjoined the shed adjacent to the main line; this shed housed locos undergoing repair, whilst those ready for traffic were stabled in the other shed.

Up to the time we left Stafford, a "bank" engine was always available to assist trains in trouble between 6.0am and 10.0pm, a 4-4-0 L.N.W. George V usually being provided for this turn, which also involved a fairly busy routine of station pilot duties. This was "top link" duty and the enginemen needed considerable route knowledge since they could be called upon to double-head trains over the Trent Valley route to London, or via Birmingham, both with possible diversions en route. In the down direction they had to be familiar with the Chester, Preston, Liverpool and Manchester roads and they always reported for duty with "double trip" baskets ready to book off away from home.

Communications were comparatively primitive and the first indication that a driver was in trouble often came after he "crowed" when passing a signalbox. As far as I can recall a "crow" was described in the Appendices to the Working Timetables as a series of short whistles followed by a long one and various meanings were ascribed to it, at different signalboxes. One can imagine the bustle of furious activity should it become necessary at short notice to take the bank engine on shed to turn it, or to replenish the tender.

Incidentally, shortly before leaving Stafford I saw my first "Royal Scot" at close quarters on the shed – it had failed on a Liverpool – Euston express due to a burst flexible steam brake pipe to the bogie brake cylinders. . . .

During our stay in Stafford I saw my paternal grandfather quite often, for the journey from his home in Crewe was only a short one. After we moved to Swansea, his visits became less frequent and he died, aged eighty, a few months after I started work in 1932. He had begun life in 1852 on a farm in Shropshire and had left home at the age of fourteen to begin work at Crewe shed, progressing through the footplate grades to be appointed Footplate Inspector (Northern Division) in 1905, retiring during 1922. He had a typically Victorian attitude towards children, who were to be seen and not heard, and he rarely spoke directly to me. "Is the lad alright?" he would ask my mother, nodding in my direction. But I was an avid listener and I now believe he was aware of this and, whilst his reminiscences were directed at my father, I think they were related for my benefit. He was a great raconteur and though his stories were not intentionally amusing, they sometimes appear so in retrospect.

My favourite is the fable about an incident during the glorious Anglo-Scottish races of 1895 between East and West Coast routes, when he was a driver in the top Crewe – Carlisle link, working an Anglo-Scottish express forward from Crewe with a 2-4-0 of the "Precedent" class. The train was 23 minutes late arriving but three minutes were regained at Crewe, thanks to some slick work during engine change. A further ten minutes had been clawed back by the time they passed Shap Summit, and now the free-running 2-4-0 was unleashed for a good gallop downhill to Carlisle Citadel station. As they approached Penrith, a gang of platelayers were seen to be carrying an enormous crossing timber over the track ahead. My grandfather blew the whistle and reached to shut the regulator, but before he could do so the engine struck the timber, which the men had dropped across the track as they leapt clear. There was a great jolt, followed by a floating, curious feeling of flying. . . . the driving wheels, released momentarily from their grip on the rails, spun sharply and the engine exhaust beats quickened dramatically. . . . then came a second jolt and the exhaust tempo returned to normal as the engine dropped safely back on the rails. . . .

The train arrived in Carlisle only seven minutes late and when examined on Upperby shed not so much as a scratch could be found on the engine. After hearing stories like this, normal railway work seemed very prosaic!

Railway employees also abounded on the maternal side of the family and one had uncles who were artisans in Crewe Works and therefore, by some strange quirk of human reasoning, considered by the townsfolk to be of superior social standing to mere "sheddies" – men who worked in the shed. An even greater social gap separated people in clerical work, a fact very much resented by my father (whose older brother was a clerk) and one which undoubtedly influenced his decision to prepare me for the Railway clerical services. He sent me to an establishment in Swansea with the sonorous title of "Pagefield College", where for over a year I was taught the disciplines necessary to pass the Railway Clerical examination – which, in the event, I failed.

When a suitable opening occurred a few months later I began work as an apprentice fitter, and suffered considerably from the fact that my father was in charge of the depot, which put him in a particularly strong position to express his displeasure with a display of rigid discipline both at home and at work.

Swansea was no more than an outpost of the L.M.S.R. buried deep in hostile G.W. territory but the shed still radiated a powerful L.N.W. aura and was considered important enough to merit District Headquarters status; perhaps the fact that it was so isolated had some bearing on this – it was 120 miles to the nearest L.M.S. loco shed of any importance at Shrewsbury. There were three sub-sheds: Llandovery, Carmarthen and Builth Road, in that order of importance. Llandovery shed was a substantial building of stone construction with a wooden roof covering four roads, typically L.N.W. in design. Its main purpose was the provision of bank engine assistance in the rear of all freight trains northbound up the notorious single line Sugar Loaf incline, which began with a 1 in 80 gradient some quarter of a mile north of the station. The ascent then varied between 1 in 80 and 1 in 70 for the next five miles to the passing loop at Cynghordy, where the real slogging began – a 4½ mile stretch of 1 in 60 up to Sugar Loaf tunnel and through the tunnel to Sugar Loaf Halt, just outside the northern portal of the tunnel.

Four ex-L.N.W. 0-8-4 7F tanks designed by Captain Hewitt Pearson Montague Beames, were supplied from Swansea for this work. Llandovery carried out the day-to-day maintenance, but the locos were returned to Swansea for heavy repairs and programmed maintenance. As a class, they were heavy on repairs and hardly a month went by without one of them running a trailing axle hot. Captain H.P.M. Beames had seen fit to equip these locomotives with mechanical lubrication to the coupled wheel axle-boxes – a laudable decision, one might think, after generations of axles lubricated by the often unpredictable capillary action of worsted wool trimmings. But unfortunately the clearance between the trailing coupled wheels and the frame, through which the axle-box oil pipes passed was so limited that when only small amounts of lateral wear developed in the trailing axleboxes, this was sufficient to permit the wheel tyres to bear against the oil pipes, which would either be worn through or quite flattened.

I can never recall seeing so cluttered a footplate as on these locomotives; crew comfort had been totally neglected to make way for a mind-boggling array of dual purpose reversing gear: lever reversing, presumably to facilitate shunting duties, and screw reversing to permit fine adjustment of valve travel when working trains. The net result was a complex arrangement of levers and pins which made lubrication almost impossible and the screw quickly became very stiff to operate. The lever quadrant had notches for only three positions: forward, mid, and reverse. The difficulty in manipulating the screw reverser meant that drivers invariably used the lever both for shunting and working trains. Instead of having the best of both modes, as was the designer's intention, they had the worst and it is devoutly to be wished that Captain Beames, who undoubtedly rejoiced in having conjured up the optimum in reversing gears, passed beyond without ever suffering the agonies of disillusionment.

The shed at Llandovery was supervised on day turn by a salaried foreman. Two "fitters in charge" looked after the remainder of the 24 hours and their duties were chiefly supervisory with only a small part of their day spent on minor running repairs. Relative to the number of engines stationed there, Llandovery had a large staff of enginemen, for as well as bank engine duties, they relieved Swansea and Shrewsbury crews on most freight trains over the Central Wales line. In addition to the Shrewsbury men who booked off at Llandovery on "double-home" trips, it is surprising nowadays to contemplate that several sets of Swansea men also booked off there each night – even though the place was only some 30 miles from Swansea. As there was no train crew lodging house, the men were accommodated in private houses. The L.M.S. paid householders 1s. 6d. for each man per night, which fee included preparation of a hot meal from food supplied by the men.

Carmarthen shed, on the other hand, was a self-contained establishment having very little contact with the outside world and, apart from the slightest brush with the "main line" at Llandilo, the staff appeared to live a most secluded life. The line from Llandilo to the Great Western station Carmarthen Town was some fifteen miles long, with the shed, a small two-road affair, some half a mile from the station alongside the G.W. line to Aberystwyth. The L.M.S. had running powers over this line from Carmarthen Town station to a point about 1½ miles to the north, where the L.M.S. single line branched to the right for its run along the Tywi valley to join the L.M.S.-G.W. joint line at Llandilo – or to use the modern spelling, Llandeilo.

Although I travelled over the line on only three or four occasions, I remember it as a beautiful run, through lush thickly-wooded countryside with the Tywi almost constantly in sight on one or other side of the line. A bridge took the tracks over the river just south of Llandilo and from there the Tywi meandered through country on the north side of the railway until reaching a spot between Llanarthney and Nantgaredig stations. There, trains crossed the river over a rather unusual high girder bridge with cross bracing members positioned just above coach roof level; viewed at a distance from the footplate as one approached it gave the impression of being too small to accept a real live train.

Three 2-4-2 1PT Webb locos were stationed at Carmarthen shed, which had staff and facilities to perform boiler washing. The shed was supervised by a fitter-in-charge who also carried out minor repairs, and the 5′ 6″ tanks (as we called them) only returned to Swansea for heavy repairs or mileage examinations. They were great little engines, free running and quite liked by enginemen; they gave us very little trouble so long as they were kept away from that treacherous stretch of sand-covered track around Swansea Bay. The only occasions they ever ran hot – boxes were after a few trips with local passenger trains between Swansea Victoria and Pontardulais.

L.M.S. passenger trains ran from the G.W. Carmarthen Town station to connect with Swansea to Shrewsbury services at Llandilo, and connecting services to Carmarthen were provided for the Shrewsbury – Swansea services.

During the summer months in pre-war days, this route was used extensively by folk from the north-west holidaying in Pembrokeshire resorts and one felt a service of through carriages between Shrewsbury and Tenby would have paid dividends.

A daily pick-up freight ran in both directions between Carmarthen and Llandilo, but perhaps the most lucrative train of all was the one that conveyed vacuum-braked fish vans from Milford Haven to connect at Llandilo with the 4/40pm "Fish" from Swansea South Dock to Crewe. This train was composed entirely of vacuum braked four-wheel vans and a guard's van, and was rostered to be worked to Crewe Gresty Lane marshalling yard by a Swansea 4-6-0 4F Whale 19″ goods. Unfortunately, so voracious was the appetite of these engines, they rarely had enough coal to go beyond Shrewsbury with a heavy train – or with one of moderate loading if the wind happened to be against them. . . .

This train also had the distinction of being the only service over the Central Wales regularly booked for assistance by bank engines in front up Sugar Loaf and between Builth Road and Llandrindod; goods trains were, of course, assisted from the rear.

A track-side mileage post just north of Builth Road station defined the limit of the Swansea Locomotive District, and the small one-road wooden engine shed was just within this boundary. North of Llandovery, the line was owned by the L.M.S. as far as Craven Arms junction, where it met the L.M.S. – G.W. joint line running between Shrewsbury and Abergavenny junction. An 0-6-0 2F Webb "Cauliflower" was shedded at Builth Road for banking, also to look after the traffic arising from the loop connection with the G.W.R. (ex-Cambrian) line which ran beneath the L.M.S. platforms, the two stations being linked by steps for interchange passengers.

This, then, was the extent of the L.M.S. Swansea Locomotive District in 1932: the 52-mile length of line from Swansea to Builth Road, the 7-mile goods-only branch line along the north Gower coast from Gowerton to Llanmorlais, and the 15-mile branch between Llandilo and Carmarthen. The Superintendent who ruled over this empire was one James R. Rowbottom, a gentleman of impeccable Crewe breeding whose favourite garb for all seasons was black coat and waistcoat, pin-striped trousers, spats over highly polished shoes, white shirt and black tie, all topped by the mandatory bowler hat; he might have been going to a funeral. Of course, that was how the Board of Directors expected their officers to dress – an outward expression of serious and dedicated commitment to the business of running a railway. But James R. Rowbottom was a man who laughed easily and often, as I well knew from several visits to his home.

Mr. and Mrs. Rowbottom lived in a block of Victorian buildings between the main line viaduct and the engine sheds. The block comprised the train crew lodging house and accommodation for the family of the steward-in-charge. Next came Mr. Rowbottom's dwelling, followed by that intended for his assistant. My father had not endeared himself by refusing to occupy this house, which had been vacated by his predecessor but Mr. Rowbottom was not the man to bear a grudge and it did not prevent him from inviting us to his Christmas parties.

Families from all sections of his staff were invited to attend, and after tea we youngsters went into the drawing room to play games with Mr. Rowbottom who, after a very short time always fell into such helpless paroxysms of laughter at our antics he was unable to rise from his chair. Every year, after about half an hour we would decide he had had enough and one of us would go the dining room, where the rest of the adults were still at table, and ask for assistance from our parents. Our fathers would come and help our half-delirious but entirely sober host back to recuperate in the dining room.

On the morning I started work, the leading fitter told me I must see Mr. Rowbottom as soon as he arrived. Accordingly, when we had changed the pony spring on 2317 I went to his office, removed my cap and tapped upon his door. "Come in!" I went inside and he gazed at me without any sign of recognition.

"Who are you, boy?" Mr. Rowbottom chortled; he had a black walrus moustache that twitched in a fascinating manner when he laughed – which he did most of the time.

"The new apprentice, sir".

"Ha! Ha! Not old Charlie's lad?"

"Yes, sir". That innocuous reply seemed to electrify the moustache.

"Ho! Ho! Well, just behave yourself – go and get on with it, boy!"

It was said of Mr. Rowbottom he laughed loudest when handing out disciplinary forms to the staff and that it was possible to deduce the severity of punishment by careful note of how quickly the moustache twitched.

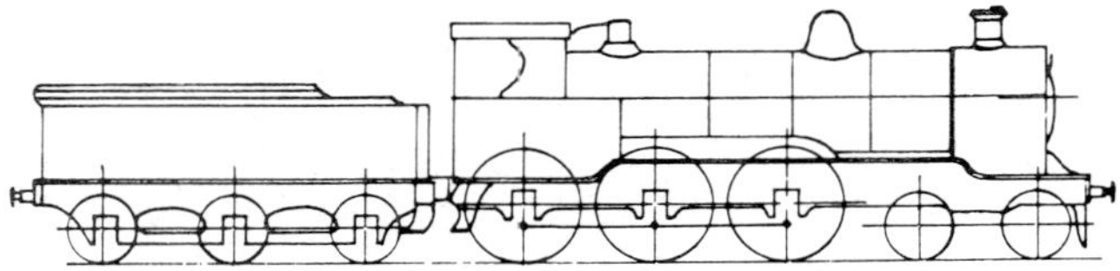

CHAPTER II

The First Year

In 1932 the engine allocation at Swansea was substantially as follows:

			Built	Driving Wheels	Designer	No. Allocated
2-4-2	1PT	L.N.W.R.	1890	5′ 8½″	Webb	4
0-6-2	2FT	L.N.W.R.	1882	4′ 5½″	Webb	7
0-6-0	2F	L.N.W.R.	1887	5′ 2½″	Webb	4
4-6-0	4F	L.N.W.R.	1908	5′ 2½″	Whale	5
0-8-2	6FT	L.N.W.R.	1911	4′ 5½″	Bowen Cooke	2
0-8-4	7FT	L.N.W.R.	1923	4′ 5½″	Beames	5
0-8-0	6F	L.N.W.R.	1904	4′ 5½″	Whale	6
0-8-0	7F	L.N.W.R.	1921	4′ 5½″	Bowen Cooke	8
0-6-0	1FT	M.R.	1878	4′ 7″	Johnson	1
0-6-0	3F	M.R.	1885	4′ 11″	Johnson	2
2-6-4	4PT	L.M.S.	1927	5′ 9″	Fowler	7
					Total	51

The fitting staff consisted of the following grades:

Leading fitter		1
Fitters		7
Apprentice fitters		2
Jointmaker		1
Fitters' mates		3
Boilersmith		1
Tuber		1
	Total	16

Three fitters on shift work covered the 24 hours and they had "passed cleaners" as their assistants. Passed cleaners of course had been passed-out for firing duties and were the senior cleaners at the depot and therefore the first on each shift to fill vacant firing turns. This was excellent training for aspiring young footplatemen and a few years later one of our chaps left the L.M.S. for an East African railway where he achieved the status of Chief Locomotive Inspector.

Three salaried running shift foremen covered the 24 hours but as these positions were traditionally the province of footplatemen without mechanical training, responsibility for mechanical matters in the absence of the leading fitter fell upon the shoulders of the three shift fitters, who were selected for their reliability.

Of the fitters on regular daywork, one was a large Cornishman accomplished in machine work who did all our turning and planed crossheads and axleboxes; in his spare time he examined once daily all the locomotives working passenger trains and once weekly all those on freight work. The machinery Reg Smith had to work with was a rare collection of antique metal work even in those days. It was belt driven from a large electric motor, through a main shaft mounted in the roof with belts to a vertical boring bar, drilling machine, planing machine, screw cutting lathe, an enormous sandstone grinding wheel and a wheel lathe for tyre turning, but without an axle journal attachment.

The electric motor driving this Heath Robinson array was started by first closing the main switch which supplied current to a huge rheostat, whereupon the motor would hum threateningly, causing men of timid nature to cower somewhat. One needed courage to take the next step of moving the rheostat, with infinite care, across all the stages of resistance until top speed was reached. There was always something of a dilemma confronting one in this situation – too slow a start would bring a shout of "Get a bloody move on!" from Reg Smith, whilst too rapid a start would either bring the main belt off its pulley or blow a fuse – in either event a rapid retreat was advisable to avoid the wrath of Mr. Smith.

One of the remaining three fitters was kept occupied dealing with hot boxes on the wheel drop and had as his fitter's mate Clarence Jones. After my first week with shift fitter Reg Jenkins, I was sent to work with fitter Phillip Spode Plant on the wheel drop – and that was when I was introduced to the practice of journal filing. We had to remove a pair of trailing coupled wheels from a Fowler 2-6-4T – a class which seemed to favour running their trailing coupled axles hot, although they were not adverse to overheating the occasional driving or leading axle by way of variety. Of course, it was much easier to "drop" the trailing pair of coupled wheels than the driving or leading – one needed to dismantle the entire set of connecting and coupling rods and the return cranks to remove the latter pairs of wheels, but with trailers one could get away with knocking out the joint pins abaft the driving wheel cranks and removing the short trailing section of coupling rods.

The predilection of L.M.S.R. locos for running hot boxes was due to inept bearing design – it was not until Stanier's advent, bringing with him Swindon ideas about axle box design and lubrication, that Derby's problems in this regard were finally solved. But the 2-6-4's predisposition for overheated trailing boxes was compounded by the very poor access to the top of these axleboxes imposed by their proximity to the firebox, which made it very difficult for fitters to inspect the condition of the rubber pipe feeding oil from the mechanical lubricator to a pressure valve on top of the axlebox – rubber pipes that were subjected to fairly intense heat from the firebox which caused them to perish and leak. After the almost statutory period of a couple of years time-lag, Derby got the message and began to supply flexible oil pipes lagged by heat-resistant asbestos sleeves. This alleviated the anguish somewhat but the cure awaited Sir William Stanier, who arrived on the scene too late to help these parallel boiler 2-6-4 tanks.

As soon as we began work on this particular loco it became obvious, even to my inexperienced eye, that the degree of overheating had been unusually severe. Paint had charred and peeled from the wheel boss, leaving the bright steel of the axle visible. Underneath, white metal had melted away from the horncheek bearing surfaces and blobs had solidified on the bearing spring top plate. There was no sign of the normal accumulations of oily grime – it had burned to a friable brown inch-thick coating that fell away in puffs of dust at a touch. The wheel set was removed and manhandled beneath the manually-operated overhead gantry, where both axleboxes were lifted off. One journal was blackened and deeply scored with heavy brass intrusion. From the remarks of the fitter one understood the wheels would have to go to Crewe Works for journal turning, a procedure taking about two weeks.

But the leading fitter had other ideas. This class was in short supply, with one of the Swansea spare engines in Derby Works and the other undergoing valve and piston examination. He handed me a 14″ "rough" flat file and told me to file out the score marks and brass intrusions, adjuring me not to put any "flats" on the journal in the process. As everyone who has ever used a file will be aware, it is much easier to file a round surface round than a flat surface flat and I managed to avoid "flats". After many inspections by the Leading Fitter, I was given a flat "smooth" file and told to remove the "rough" file marks. Finally, the journal had to be polished with grades of emery cloth ranging from coarse to very fine. The other apprentice and myself were shown how to interlock sheets of emery round the journal beneath coils of spun yarn, doubled and wound in a manner which allowed us to pull at the ends like men using a cross-cut saw, always keeping the rope taut and the emery cloth well lubricated with paraffin. The entire process took three or four days and by the time it was finished the axlebox and bearing had been re-metalled, planed and bored and only needed fitting to the journal.

It was usual practice to give a re-fitted axlebox one day running-in on light duties before committing the engine to normal work. The 8.30a.m. local passenger from Swansea to Pontardulais, returning with a pick-up goods which also served the Gowerton-Llanmorlais branch, was the turn used for the purpose and we went to meet the engine when it returned to shed that afternoon. The bearing temperatures were normal so it was allowed to return to rostered work and there is little doubt the same axle lasted until Beeching arrived to give steam the Great Heave-Ho.

This was by no means the only wheel journal filed at Swansea during the early days of my apprenticeship, but it was the worst case, and one knows of other similarly isolated sheds which occasionally followed the same very reprehensible procedure.

At an engine shed the size of Swansea, there was insufficient work to warrant the employment of a full time coppersmith or whitemetaller and fitters had to perform the work. Reg Smith had served an apprenticeship as a machinist and turner, but after he left the depot for promotion in 1935, this duty also fell to the fitters. At the larger sheds and main works apprentice fitters were put with these tradesmen during their training but never had to put the teaching into practice, as we at Swansea did. Wheel drop fitter Plant was our expert metaller but the business of standing near by when he was at work could be a rather traumatic experience, as will be explained later.

Some of the axleboxes we dealt with were of integral design: the journal bearing was part of the axlebox, not a separate "step" which could be removed. Instead, three brass strips some 3″ wide were dovetailed into the axlebox crown: one at the top of the semicircle, drilled for oilways, with two other strips each at 90° angles from the vertical, and between these strips was the whitemetal bearing surface. It will be appreciated that, whilst it may have been necessary only to renew the fused white metal in the journal bearing, it was impossible to do so without melting the white metal off the axlebox horncheek and wheelboss in the process. This necessitated the renewal of all the white metal, but we had no "formers" or moulds which could be secured around the axlebox after tinning, into which molten metal could be poured and allowed to cool before removing the former. The white metal had literally to be "pasted" on to all the surfaces, using suitably shaped wooden pasting sticks that we apprentices made from discarded shunting poles or brake sticks. The whitemetalling was done on an open coke-fired hearth with forced draughting, which also served for brazing copper pipes. After heating the axlebox to remove the unwanted white metal the next process was to clean thoroughly or tin all surfaces to be metalled with a particularly obnoxious flux supplied in hard blocks of white material which had to be hammered into powder before it could be used. When applied to hot metal, dense clouds of white gas rose to the roof; one could guarantee that no birds roosted in the rafters when we were metalling.

White bearing metal came in 14lb ingots, identified by the cryptic symbols WM1, WM2, & WM3, denoting the surfaces on which it should be used. It was an alloy of tin, antimony, copper and lead, and resistance to wear increased proportionately to its tin content. Unfortunately, so did the price, and for that reason WM1, containing the greatest tin content, was restricted to use on the highest load-bearing surfaces such as big end bearings. WM2 and WM3 were intended for use on surfaces of progressively lighter loadings, and contained less tin.

The temperature of white metal and the surface to be metalled was critical to the process of pasting. When adequately tinned, the axlebox would be positioned with journal bearing area horizontal and the work of pasting the more difficult vertical horncheek and wheel boss surfaces would be completed first, leaving the journal bearing until last: this area was in the thickest part of the axlebox and would retain its heat longest. If either the axlebox or the white metal were too hot it would simply run off the surface. If either were below the required temperature the metal would not adhere correctly, but this defect would often not be discovered until the machining process had reached an advanced stage, when the first intimation of disaster would be a roar of anger from the machinist.

Everybody agreed it was a cliff-hanging experience to stand and observe the technique of Phillip S. Plant as he metalled; obviously one sweated copious amounts in all that heat but he seemed to have a nose specially shaped to guide all the facial perspiration to its end, where it gathered in droplets of increasing size, until they were suspended above the ladle of molten metal in his hand like the proverbial sword of Damocles. . . . Anyone who has witnessed the result of water droplets falling on molten metal will know of the miniature explosion which follows – spraying tiny molten particles everywhere, landing on bare skin with an effect far more painful than the sting of a wasp. But Phillip would shape his lips in a special way and blow them off just before they reached critical size and never once did he allow one to fall into the molten metal.

Before an axlebox could be machined it was imperative to establish the centre point of the axle relative to the mainframe horncheeks. On

L.M.S. locomotives built prior to the Stanier era it could never be assumed that a point equidistant from each horncheek was where the centreline of an axle should be. This arose from the questionable L.M.S. main works practice of allowing differing thickness of metal to be ground off worn horncheeks, providing that parallelism was maintained, and to enable running shed staff to cope with this extraordinary situation data was provided in the form of a "centre pop" mark on the main frame each side of the horncheeks. A point equidistant from the centre pops was the axle centre line, and this data needed to be transferred to axleboxes to enable them to be machined accurately.

After planing the horncheek surfaces to size, our machinist always insisted we should man-handle the axlebox up the locomotive horncheeks into its normal working position for marking-off purposes. A little thought convinces one this arduous procedure was quite unnecessary – by careful measurement the same result could be achieved with the axlebox on the bench; but habit dies hard, and a couple of years went by before the light dawned at Swansea.

Such practices were anathema to G.W. locomotive engineers, who believed it wiser to spend more time and money to ensure the centre line of their horncheeks remained at the same geometric point throughout the life of a locomotive.

I was unaware of this when I returned to Swansea as mechanical foreman in 1946 and remained unenlightened until after Nationalisation, when we became part of the Western Region's Neath Motive Power District. Some time later we got ourselves snowed under by hot boxes and the District Mechanical Inspector offered to help by taking an L.M.S. locomotive to Danygraig for repairs. This depot had been the main Locomotive and C.&.W. workshop of the old Rhondda & Swansea Bay Railway, but by this time the staff had become deeply inured in G.W. practices. I sent one of our 2-6-4 tanks there to have attention to a hot trailing axlebox, and when it returned a few days later, it was put on our running-in job – the 8.30 Swansea – Pontardulais local passenger train, during which it proceeded to run the metal out of both trailing coupling rod bushes. The more discerning reader will have divined the cause of this, but one freely admits it was not until we tried to replace the trailing coupling rods with their bushes remetalled and bored and found we could not do so, that we began to realise what had taken place. We could get one side coupling rod on, but the other bush was a good 1/8″ or 3/16″ from slipping over the crank pin and it was established that Danygraig had used the centre point between horncheeks as their datum to bore out the axle bearings, with a result the entire wheel set had been moved forward approximately ¼″!

The Neath inspector was advised and when the wheels were removed, he came along and watched as we demonstrated the purpose of these main frame datum marks, shaking his head in total disbelief at such weird goings-on. What puzzled us most was how the Danygraig staff managed to get the coupling rods on at all – ever since I have suspected that some very nefarious G.W. method was used!

The type which gave most trouble were the Webb 0-6-2T coal engines, known as "Gadgets" in the Swansea District. They had a higher frequency of hot axles and their motion parts, particularly the piston crosshead slide blocks and little ends, wore out at an alarming rate. All of this could be laid at the door of the "Vacuum Controlled Regulator" (or V.C.R.) equipment that enabled them to work Push-and-pull services between Swansea and Pontardulais. They propelled the two coach suburban sets from the latter town and, as a result, the Gadgets received the full benefit of the clouds of fine sand stirred up by the preceding coaches between Mumbles Road and Swansea Bay stations. The situation became so bad that as they passed through Crewe Works for programmed overhaul, special plates were fitted beneath the slide bars in an effort to exclude the sand. Needless to say, they proved worse than useless, creating a pressure drop above the plates which had the opposite effect from that intended and caused sand to be deposited to a depth of several inches on the plating. This effect could be plainly seen from the footframing if one cared to ride in that somewhat precarious position across the "sands". In addition, the plates were an impediment to both inspection and maintenance, and as soon as each Gadget arrived "fresh off works", we pounced upon them at once and removed the plating.

Different methods of push and pull working were in use – the G.W.R. used mechanical linkages between loco regulator and coach, whilst certain pre-Grouping railways adopted compressed air cylinders for this purpose. But the L.M.S. developed a very sophisticated, and probably the most expensive system of all, involving as it did the fitting of an entirely separate regulator valve in the main steam pipe between smokebox header and cylinders, plus a vacuum cylinder mounted outside on the footframing to operate it – and if the engine had outside cylinders, as on the 2-6-2 3P tank, the whole gubbins had to be duplicated.

The intended method of regulator control from a coach driving compartment was that whilst working in push and pull mode the main regulator should remain open and control of steam admitted to the cylinders was then vested in the driver's vacuum control regulator valve, to which was connected a vacuum gauge, in theory registering an infinite choice of regulator valve positions between closed (0″ h.g.) and fully opened (21″ h.g.). But it did not work like this, as I can attest from several trips on the footplates of the "Gadgets", whose V.C.R. cylinders had pistons with leather sealing washers which needed regular dosage with castor oil if they were to work at all. Footplatemen had learned from bitter experience that this cylinder gave but two positions – open or shut, with nothing in between. They had devised a simple method to deal with this: when at a station the fireman kept an eye on the V.C.R. vacuum gauge and as soon as he saw the finger move away from the zero position he would open the regulator and as speed increased, alter the opening to suit demand and adjust valve travel as necessary. Of course, even with V.C.R. that operated satisfactorily he would still have to perform the latter function and look after the regulator when wheel slip occurred – it was doubtful if the driver would be aware of wheel slip from two coaches distant. The system was designed to fail-safe and fortunately the vacuum controlled regulator valve always closed satisfactorily by operating the valve in the coach driving compartment. There was also an electric bell code system between coach and footplate, and a mechanical linkage to the loco whistle if all else failed. The pistons of V.C.R. cylinders were sealed by rubber diaphragms in later versions fitted to 2-6-2 3P tanks and gave much better control of valve openings.

The number of hot axles on the Gadgets could have been reduced, had Mr. Webb insisted on an oilbox design aimed at excluding the ingress of dirt but, as was usually the case with L.N.W. locos, this had been sacrificed for cheapness and simplicity.

A story, probably apocryphal, has it that Churchward, when confronted by the G.W. Board of Directors with the far cheaper L.N.W. building costs for comparable locomotives, replied curtly that one of his would last twice as long and pull twice as much as one of theirs. History has proved Mr. Churchward wrong in the first of those claims and the second is controversial; he should have laid claim to undeniably superior design. . . .

The lubrication of both the leading and driving coupled wheel axleboxes on the Gadgets consisted of two oil wells forged into the crown of the axlebox. Two taper brass plugs, approximately 1¼″ dia. by 3″ long, passed through the axlebox crown to secure the brass bearing "step" in position, and each plug was drilled with a ¼″ dia. hole to receive a worsted wool trimming, with its feeder strands submerged in the oil wells. Laminated springs were sited above these axles, with a circular pillar located beneath the spring buckle and centrally on the crown of the axlebox. An 1/8" thick plate, shaped to the contour of the horncheeks and drilled with 3/8" holes for the spout of an oil can, plus one of 1½" dia. for the spring pillar, acted as a lid covering the axlebox top and its oil wells. It was held in position by a weak coil spring in compression between the lid and the bottom spring pillar guide bracket and, because of restrictions imposed by this bracket, the lid could be raised by no more than two inches, which was insufficient to allow us to clean the oil wells except by positioning the wheels on the "drop" table and lowering them until the axlebox underkeep rested on the horncheek clips. But this only worked with the leading wheels: with the innate perverseness of inanimate objects, one could guarantee when we tried it with the driving pair the big end sweeps would bar our way. We knew it would be useless to ask a driver to run the "Gadget" outside and slip the wheels for us – they were always in exactly the same position when we got it back on the drop table.

Hot axles on our Gadgets usually afflicted leading or driving wheel sets – the trailing coupled wheels were supplied with oil from splendid oil boxes on the footplate through flexible pipes. Fortunately the leading wheel sets were child's play to remove: six taper pins to be knocked out of the push-fit collars on the crank pins – a quick jerk at each end of the side-rods and they would be on the floor. Eight brake pull rod pins to be removed and the pull rods rested neatly beside the side-rods. Underneath there were four 5/8" bolts to remove from flanges at each end of the 2½" dia. main vacuum pipe, and four 1" bolts from the horncheek clips. Every part was dismantled so frequently that nuts spun off at a touch and pins leapt out at the mere sight of a hammer. Forty minutes was the sort of time Fitter Plant allowed from starting work to lowering a leading wheel set down the "drop" well, with perhaps ten minutes of that waiting for the shed turner to come along with an engine and shunt us on and off the drop table. The term shed turner was applied to the driver and fireman on each shift who were responsible for turning, fire cleaning, coaling, watering and stabling each locomotive as it arrived on shed, and for moving locomotives to the requirements of maintenance staff.

The axlebox bearings on the Gadgets were of the brass "step" variety, being removed from the axlebox by first knocking out the two tapered brass securing plugs, and then by using a suitably dimensioned stretcher bolt between the axlebox legs. Only on very rare occasions was white metal on the axlebox itself affected by overheating – drivers kept a very close watch on the axleboxes of these engines and because of the nature of their duties it was usually possible to withdraw them from traffic before any serious damage was done.

Cast of soft brass, the bearing step had four diagonal pockets filled with white metal each side at 45 degrees from the vertical to take piston thrust loadings. Another pocket was cast in line with the axle at the top of the bearing to receive the two tapered brass oil plugs and was, presumably, expected to act as an oil reservoir. It was important to replace the remetalled "step" back in the axlebox before fitting it on to the journal, since releasing the "stretcher" bolt between the axlebox legs would have a slightly compressive effect on the semi-circular shape of the bearing step. Refitting was always done completely by hand on "Gadget" axle bearings, using the time honoured method of scraping with an assortment of scrapers laboriously fashioned in bull-nose, half-round and a variety of other shapes from worn-out files.

A recipe of red-lead and engine oil was used to make a paste of "raddle", spread thinly around the journal for marking high spots on the bearing. The desired end product was a bearing whereon most of the load was distributed evenly upon the white metal of each pocket with only the slightest hint of red raddle on the brass bearing areas. Additionally, it was considered imperative to provide a ¼″ lead area of very slight taper at both edges of the crown pocket in order to achieve an even distribution of oil along the journal in either direction of travel. Traditionally, this work was left to the apprentices under the supervision of leading fitter Harry Kay, and when we believed we had achieved perfection he would be invited to inspect our work. He would always begin by wiping off all the paste on the journal, replacing it with a mere suggestion of raddle. Next he ensured none remained on the bearing before telling us to drop the axlebox in position. Then he would push it, pull it, bang it from side to side – and even try to "rock" it on the journal. Often, his reduction in the thickness of raddle on the journal would produce markings on the bearing like miniature mountain peaks poking through cloud cover, and we would have to start all over again, scraping to much finer limits this time.

My fellow apprentice had started work a few months before myself but we enrolled together in August 1932 for the winter Mechanical Engineering course at Swansea Technical College. In those days railway artisan grades were treated very much as a necessary but rather undesirable appendage of the organisation. The only travel concessions allowed us were tickets at quarter fare rates, and one could only obtain a free ticket as a reward for attending a winter session of eighteen Sunday afternoon ambulance classes, followed by an examination pass.

Paid annual holidays did not begin until 1938 and prior to that at Swansea all the fitting staff were paid off without pay on Christmas Day and Good Friday and so the chances of apprentices being allowed time concessions to attend evening classes were zero. We worked a 47 hour week, finishing at 5/30p.m. on weekdays, which gave one an hour and a quarter before classes began, three nights each week. My fellow sufferer was in a worst position than myself – he lived in Mumbles some four miles west of Swansea and how he managed to pedal home, wash, change, dine and get back to Tech. in that time was always a source of wonderment to me.

The posts of lecturers to evening classes at Swansea Tech must have been spare time jobs then, since I recall that our favourite, who took us in Engineering Science, was employed at the recently commissioned Tir John power station. He was a man of infectious enthusiasm who took pains to imbue his students with the same spirit, even to the extent of organising a Sunday morning visit to Tir John for those of us who were interested. He also arranged visits to the workshops of Palmers Dry Dock, and to the enginerooms of several vessels in Swansea Docks.

Next year, when we enrolled at Tech, it was to find this lecturer had left, and with him went much of one's own enthusiasm for night school.

At the beginning of 1933 I was put with Reg Smith, who taught me how to use the various machines – all, that is, except the great tyre-turning wheel lathe which, to the best of one's recollection, was never used at all. It was quite fascinating to discover how to assemble screw-cutting gear trains with sprockets having the correct number of teeth necessary to produce the required number of threads per inch, and if the latter number was odd, how to ensure the gear was synchronized before beginning a cut. This was achieved by an apparently esoteric ritual wherein one chalked in-line spokes on both the driving and lead screw sprockets, and it was essential these were in phase before engaging the tool rest with the lead screw.

This lathe was too small to bore axleboxes; anything larger than a pair of big-end brasses had to be machined on the table of our "vertical boring bar" – a piece of equipment remarkable only for its antiquity. In order to bore a bearing it was necessary first to assemble the axlebox around the bar, on the slotted steel surface plates, fitting the underkeep into position before setting the journal bearing concentric to the boring bar, which was slotted to receive tools ½″ × 3″ in section, and of varying length. These were locked *in situ* by gib and cotter, and secured by a set-screw. The downward feed of the cut was automatic, but could only be increased by slacking the set-screw and tapping the tool out of its slot a little further after each pass – a "hit and miss" method which produced many machining errors. Tight bearings could be fitted by hand, but slack ones inevitably led to many instances of axle bearing knock. Poor finish of bearing surfaces was an unavoidable consequence of the overlong extension of the boring bar between its upper and lower bearings, which allowed it to whip, and produced undercutting of the softer white metal to leave the harder brass surfaces standing proud. This was precisely the opposite of what was required of any bearing and left a lot of hand scraping still to be done.

Later that year I went to work with fitter Jack Lewis, whose birthplace was Nantwich, a small market town just west of Crewe. To Swansea's many immigrant Crewe railwaymen he was known as "Dabber" Lewis (that was the title they bestowed on all Nantwichers) but we apprentices found a more suitable nickname – "Slogger" Lewis, because of his attitude to work in general and big hammers in particular. Even in those days, when the Protestant work ethic still had credibility and fairly hard manual work was a normal activity for the lower classes, he stood head and shoulders above most for the energy he devoted to it.

He was our valve, piston and motion expert; big and little ends, slideblocks and crossheads, pistons and cylinder covers – anything which involved heavy lifting or swinging a sledge hammer was meat and drink to Jack Lewis. At that time an enormous sledge hammer was kept at the shed for the use of anyone who could heft the thing – it must have weighed 30 or 40 lbs, and it gained for Jack Lewis his title "Slogger." Only he ever used it, reserving it for stubborn piston rods which refused to part from their crossheads under the normal persuasion of a 14 lb. hammer.

Loco piston rods had coned ends which mated into identically coned sockets in the crosshead, or slideblock. These tapers, which were in the order of 1 in 18, were drawn together by a large tapered cotter driven by sledge hammer through matching slots in piston rod cone and crosshead socket. This resulted in a fit which could only be freed (after removing the cotter) by the action of a stout steel wedge driven up to force cone and socket apart. On inside cylinder types the wedge had to be driven upwards from beneath the loco, and to an extent dependent on pit depth and one's own stature, one had to crouch low when swinging the sledge hammer. There were several hammer swinging techniques available, and for a time I favoured that which involved standing sideways on to the target, thereby permitting a greater degree of back-swing – as advocated by all golf pros. Unfortunately, whilst this was by far the most stylish action to watch, it had the disadvantage of producing a higher number of misses than that used by most other virtuosos, who stood face-on and swung the hammer upwards from between the legs.

After a while one was forcibly restrained from using the side-ways stance by one's colleagues, who claimed it was too dangerous to their life and limb.

We called this process "shooting" a crosshead because the separation of cone from socket happened suddenly, with a loud crack of noise that signalled a need to leap clear as the heavy steel wedge clattered into the pit; it was not the sort of work for those of delicate nature!

But Jack Lewis was an impatient individual not prepared to allow us to batter away with a fourteen pounder for very long before ordering one of us to "get th'big'un". Th' big'un was just about as much as I could carry but "Slogger" would perform the palm-spitting ritual and then swing it with hardly more visible effort than he used to swing the fourteen pounder. Of course, we onlookers had no objection to that – in fact, we rather enjoyed the spectacle. What we objected to was what would happen if a dozen or so earth-quaking blows proved ineffective, when we knew he would proffer the thing to one of us as though he was doing us a favour. . . .

"Ere – 'ave a bash", he would say, smiling generously. Realising we would have to do something about this before we were both rendered sexually impotent by ruptures, we apprentices hit upon the idea of hiding th'big'un in coal at the back of the tender of a Crewe-based 0-8-0, after which it was seen no more. . . .

The next fitter I worked with was a Manxman whose surname and fair complexion left one in no doubt as to his Nordic ancestry. Working with Douglas Drewsen for a few months was enough to convince me that he had come from a long line of Berserkers, for that was the spirit in which he attacked every task he was given and nothing was too hot or too heavy for Douglas to handle. He always welcomed the sort of job everyone else steered clear of – for example, smokebox jobs.

Every morning when we arrived, the night shift fitter would be standing near the time card clock, waiting for the magic moment when the hands reached eight so he could stamp his card and go home, but in the few moments before then he would convey news of the night's happenings to us; words like "I've stopped 9305 for leaking element tube joints" were enough to make everyone except Doug Drewsen run for cover, so filthy was the task of working in a smokebox. But whilst others thought up little schemes to delay the moment of going to the office for their duties, or memorised glib excuses to explain why smokebox work would be injurious to them, he'd slip into his overalls like a flash, dash to the office and plead to be given the job; plainly there had also been a hint of masochism in Doug's forebears. . . .

L.N.W. superheater element tube joints were prone to steam leakage. A steel collar was welded to the end of each steam tube with a V groove machined in the upper surface and a matching groove in the smokebox header, between which was fitted a suitably shaped copper jointing ring. This assemblage was secured to the header by a single T headed 1″ diameter bolt which slid into a slot in the header casting. In this environment of extreme temperature fluctuations copper was an unsuitable jointing material and eventually it was modified to the L.M.S. arrangement, with hemispherical ends on the tubes and mating hemispheres in the header.

Whilst it was possible to establish that element tube joints were blowing during a steam test, it was necessary to carry out a water test in order to pinpoint the offending joints and this was done during the boiler cooling-down process; when the boiler was full of water the regulator valve was opened to allow water to run through the superheated steam element tubes into the cylinders.

Mr. Drewsen was also very much at home on top of the boilers of L.N.W. 0-8-0 goods locomotives (known as Super Ds in South Wales) working on their main regulator valves, into which had been designed a propensity for steam leakage. The designer must have been a thoughtful man who had obviously anticipated this, for he had gone to the trouble of providing a neat socket, riveted on the dome plating, into which could be slipped a splendid little crane that he had specially designed to lift the dome cover off its studs and swing it clear.

This regulator valve was of the poppet type, but with coned seatings top and bottom. Such a design will produce a much larger port opening than a flat slide valve for a much smaller movement of the regulator handle. This could have disastrous consequence, as was often illustrated after Nationalisation, when occasionally they fell into the hands of inexperienced G.W.R. drivers, who naturally used the same technique with these regulator valves as they did on G.W. engines. But with a boiler water level anywhere near the top of the gauge glass, anything more than merely cracking open the regulator valve on a Super D would lift water into the main steam pipe and down into the cylinders, where havoc would be wrought.

Occasionally, if steam was seen to be issuing in moderate amounts from the cylinder cocks of Super Ds when the regulator was shut, we could rectify this by grinding in the valve with emery powder. More often it was necessary to renew the entire assembly of valve and casting complete – which involved certain other complications. With a valve of this type it was imperative the regulator handle should never be allowed to come up against the "closed" position stop on the quadrant – with its valve closed there should be an inch clearance between the handle and the "closed" stop. This was necessary to ensure that the valve would continue to close satisfactorily as wear developed in the pins and bushes of the actuating gear, or as the coned valve seatings wore. This problem was not encountered with flat slide-valve regulators, but with L.N.W. valves invariably we had to adjust the length of the valve lifting spindle to suit each new assemblage, due to differences in castings.

The L.M.S. employed a semi-skilled artisan grade known as "jointmaker", which was later changed to Fitter Grade 3 without any alteration in duties: they performed such straightforward tasks as renewing brake blocks, rejointing front cylinder covers, boiler dome covers and safety valve covers. Our jointmaker was in his sixties and a character in the very best sense of the word, and he had a pair of magical tools – a cold chisel and a long-handled adze.

If there was no Grade 3 work for him he would have to revert to fitter's mate grade, losing a proportion of the few shillings he received each week for Grade 3 work, commensurate with the time spent as a fitter's mate. This was a great incentive for the fitters to find jobs for him and we always got him to remove and replace dome covers. It was sometimes very interesting to watch him at work, particularly so when he encountered hexagon nuts whose corners had been so eroded that spanners slipped around them; without further ado out came this magic chisel and with no more than four or five blows from his hammer, a 7/8" Whitworth nut would split open as clean as a whistle, leaving not a mark on the threads of the stud.

About this time certain of our Super Ds began to appear fresh-off shops in a new guise, with 175 lb. p.s.i. boilers which meant that, with the extra 15 lb. pressure, they could now haul an additional six loaded wagons up the Sugar Loaf. During this rebuild they were also fitted with three vacuum brake cylinders to replace the solitary steam brake cylinder which had applied the brakes on both engine and tender, through a nightmarish system of rods, levers and triangular castings beneath the footplate.

Nothing else had been altered on these locomotives and the Drawing Office staff certainly must have believed that all other parts were quite capable of absorbing the additional loadings. But from then on our jointmaker was never again short of work in his own grade, for the front cylinder cover joints began to blow with such regularity that drivers came to accept that if they wanted to see a signal ahead they had to shut the regulator first. Designed for 160 lbs. p.s.i., the spacings of the front cylinder covers studs in the cylinder castings were too far apart to prevent the copper joints being blown out by the additional fifteen p.s.i. of steam pressure.

The jointmaker was also skilled in the use of an adze and for him the fitting of new wooden brake blocks to the tenders of our four "Cauliflowers" presented no problem. They were fashioned of very hard wood and had three 1″ holes drilled in the braking surface, which were filled with a resinous material to improve the braking effect and reduce the risk of fire. However, they were not shaped to match the coning of tyres, nor were they supplied in sizes to fit different tyre thicknesses, as were cast iron brake blocks. They had to be shaped on the spot to suit the wheels of individual tenders, and the only person who could do that quickly and easily was the jointmaker, with his magic adze. He would trap the brake-block beneath a foot and begin chipping small, neat flakes of wood from its surfaces until it slid sweetly up between wheel and hanger, fitting perfectly. On the rare occasion when fitters had to renew these brakeblocks the adze seemed to lose its magical properties, and to use it was to risk losing at least a toe. We held the things in a vice and used a 14″ rasp to remove unwanted wood – a lengthy and most unrewarding task.

As our "Crab" tanks lost their pristine newness, some movement began to develop in the bottom plates of the side tanks, at the point where there was a sharp reduction in tank depth just above the driving wheels, and bolts in the base of the tank at this point began to leak. Fitters seemed incapable of effecting repairs to last more than a few trips before water leaks recurred. They made jointing washers to slip under the ¾″ bolt heads out of all sorts of material – rubber, and "Walker-rite," and carbonised asbestos cord wound round the bolt shank – all these and many more were tried without avail until, in desperation, the leading fitter asked the jointmaker to have a go. A few days later, when a "Crab" 2-6-4T was stopped for leaking tank bolts, I was appointed as his aid, and as a large girth precluded his passage through the tank filler lid, I went in there to secure the bolt heads whilst he undid the nuts outside, and then I passed the bolts to him. From the pocket of his overalls he produced a neatly bound parcel and, glancing round to ensure he wasn't over-looked, he opened it and took out several reddish, greasy looking objects which he proceeded to slip over the shank of each bolt in a very furtive manner, finally passing them up to me. I gazed at the sticky mess. "What are they made of?"

"None of your business, boyo!" he replied curtly. "Just you stick them in the holes and make sure the heads don't turn when I tighten the nuts up!"

This material lasted much longer than any which had preceded it and, so secretive was the jointmaker about its composition, several months went by before the fitters discovered its true nature – and even then they were never able to reproduce all its qualities. Perhaps that was because they would not go to the trouble, as he had, of obtaining discarded lengths of tarred rope-ends from ships' chandlers, shredding them into cord to make neatly bound grommets which he would soak overnight in a concoction of red lead and linseed oil in the kitchen at home. . . .

When I asked where he had learned to use an adze so expertly he explained it was during his youth, when he had used this tool to shape trunks of Scandinavian pine into masts and spars for square riggers, whilst employed as a "chippy" at a firm of ship repairers on Swansea's long since abandoned North dock. He had not learned to make grommets there – he'd asked a labourer to show him how to do that; this labourer kept the floors of the shed and pits clean – really clean, which meant he rarely stopped working, except to light a stubby clay pipe or visit the loo.

Although a name was written on his time card for all to see, nobody could pronounce it, for it was thought to be Scandinavian, and the English version was a mere approximation. He was an old man with a severe limp and he'd been doing the same job for longer than anyone could remember. He was not the sort of person who called attention to himself, and people whom I asked about his background seemed surprised I had bothered to do so. He'd managed to draw a cloak of anonymity about himself that I found intriguing, and quite impossible to penetrate, however hard I tried to coax him. He probably thought I was mad, for I bought him several ounces of thick twist, which he first chewed, then placed the cuds in a tin box to dry out ready for smoking. But nothing worked and all I learned was no more than he'd already made known: how he'd been put ashore at Swansea in 1888, after a fall from the rigging had broken his hip in the Bay of Biscay – the ship was a barque with copper ore for the smelters in Swansea, loaded in Iquique – and this was all that I, or anyone else could discover. Press him too hard about his early life, or ask the country of his origin an odd gleam would appear in his eyes which boded ill. What strange, dark happening had caused this overwhelming need for secrecy? Perhaps it was a great joke for him to keep everyone guessing – especially young nosey parkers like myself? Or had he been crazed by his fall, as some believed?

For a few weeks that year I went to work with the shift fitters, who looked after the "running repairs" on engines – that is to say they attended to any work reported by the drivers who had brought the locomotive to the shed on completion of its work. Hardly any driver would fail to enter "brakes need adjusting" or "sand valves need opening" on a Repairs Card for an engine which had just worked over the Central Wales, and usually defects were of a minor nature concerning steam leakages from steam valve glands on the footplate, or pipe joints. L.N.W. engine brake adjustment demanded the cooperation of fitter and mate, since pins and rods had to be uncoupled. On L.N.W. tenders with compensated brake rigging it was necessary for the assistant to hold the leading and middle brake blocks against the wheels with two long wooden "spikes" before proper adjustment could be effected. The driver's brake application valves on certain L.N.W. locomotives were mounted high on the firebox faceplate, so that drivers of small stature needed to stand up to operate them. There were two valve elements, one on each side of the faceplate, coupled by a rod. The left-hand valve controlled the admission of air to the bottom side of the vacuum brake cylinders, whilst the right-hand one controlled the steam supply to the ejectors. It was a contrivance of rather clumsy appearance which seemed to work quite well, except there was no provision for quick release of vacuum on the top, or reservoir, side of the cylinders, and before we could adjust the brakes it was necessary to uncouple a small pipe leading to the reservoir side of the duplex vacuum gauge, thereby admitting equalising air to the top of the cylinders.

The method of adjusting the brakes on a Super D with the single steam brake cylinder was quite complex. One had to make allowances for the relative movement which occurred between engine and tender under buffing and drawbar loads when adjusting the tender brake pull rod, and also ensure the intermediate drawgear was not under compressive loading during adjustment.

Two types of vacuum brake cylinders were fitted to our "Gadgets": some had standard 23″ cylinders fitted in the normal way, but the majority were equipped with horizontally mounted cylinders. A chain was attached to the piston rod and passed over a pulley which converted this lateral movement to the vertical one required to lift the lever on a brake shaft which was common to both types. The problem was to keep the pulley wheel bracket secure on its studs, also to keep the spindle lubricated, for apart from a small oil hole drilled in the wheel boss there was no other way to oil the bearing. So difficult was the access that drivers ignored it, or perhaps were not even aware of its existence. The power losses caused by this layout were such that footplatemen often found the handbrake more efficacious than the power brake. The driver's "brake application valve" on these locomotives typified the low-cost simplicity of design so characteristic of the Webb era, but to call it a "valve" imparts to it an undeserved dignity: it was merely a hinged flap with a rubber sealing washer, set in the run of main vacuum pipe along the side tank on the footplate.

We had two ex-M.R. 0-6-0 Class 3F, Nos. 3389 and 3657. Whilst their building dates were comparable with the "Cauliflowers", their design was superior in every respect and they had, for shunting purposes at least, the advantage of lever reversing. This was much appreciated by drivers who had been accustomed to the 26 turns of reversing wheel required to change the direction of travel of a "Cauliflower".

These M.R. locos had brakegear operated by a separate cylinder under both engine and tender, and the steam supply to the latter cylinder was carried by a stretch of heavy gauge copper pipe between engine and tender which must have been ten or twelve feet in length, to give it the flexibility necessary to negotiate curves. At the loco end it was secured by a three-bolt flange, whilst at the tender end it was free to slide inside a gland, thus catering for the fore and aft movement which is normal between engines and tenders. One presumes this design came before the advent of flexible steam pipes but, if our experience with it was common to all similar types on the Midland, they have my heartfelt sympathy. We removed the pipes for annealing every couple of weeks, but this did not stop them breaking off at the flange and with an almost predictable frequency. The resultant escape of steam would also impair the efficiency of the engine brake cylinder to such an extent drivers would dispose of the train and return light engine to the shed, where a spare pipe was always available. Replacement probably took no more than twenty minutes.

I was working on running repairs with fitter Reg Jenkins when he was given a driver's repair card for a Super D which had just arrived on shed after working an overnight goods from Shrewsbury. During the driver's examination when finishing with the engine, he had discovered an overheated big end and had reported it. For all their other faults (and there were many), a hot big end on a Super D was unheard of, for the journals of the inside cranks were of ample dimensions, and the bearings well-designed.

When the engine was stabled in the shed, leading fitter Kay accompanied us as we entered the pit and went under the engine to inspect the big end. The L.N.W. 0-8-0, 0-8-2T and 0-8-4T had identical wheels, cylinders and motions, and they all had variations of Joy's valve gear.

The split big end brasses slid into a U-shaped steel "strap", the legs of the U then sliding over the matching end of the connecting rod. This assemblage was held together by a heavy tapered steel "fast" cotter driven down (by the inevitable 14 lb. sledge hammer) through matching slots in the strap, and it was then secured by two case-hardened 7/8" set screws and a small split cotter hammered into a rectangular hole provided in the "fast" cotter. A second, somewhat smaller cotter with one flat side was also driven down through slots and secured in the same manner as the "fast" cotter, but its purpose was to hold the split big end brasses together.

In those days, when knock or excessive wear was found in big end split brasses at strip-down examinations, it was accepted depot practice to correct this by filing an equal thickness of metal off the horns of the semi-circular brasses; effectively, this would reduce the diameter of the bearing in the load-bearing areas, but it would also introduce a degree of ovallity. The diameter of the big-end journal would be established by using outside calipers, and this measurement was then transferred to inside calipers for assessing the wear in the assembled big end brasses on the bench. The lower leg of the caliper was held firmly on the bottom of the bearing, and the upper leg moved in a radial direction to establish its amount of travel. One-eighth of an inch travel was allowed for each inch of journal, e.g: for a five inch journal, five-eighths inch travel would be acceptable, and anything above this would indicate a degree of knock, necessitating either filing or remetalling and reboring. Whilst the latter method was *de rigueur* for the heavily-loaded inside cylinder big ends of Scots, Patriots, etc., we knew we could get away with filing the ends of the brasses on Super Ds.

But to return to the over-heated big end: during dismantling we found great difficulty in getting the brasses off the journal, and eventually it dawned upon us that the crank axle "sweeps" had actually moved together and pinched the brasses, thus causing overheating at their radii.

These crank axles were of the built-up variety – that is to say they were not forged from the solid, but consisted of nine separate components, each secured to its adjacent member by interference fit under hydraulic pressure. The designer realised some movement could occur in this assemblage, for on the ends of the big end sweeps, and on the ends of their counterbalances, he had provided centre pop marks into which could be fitted special matching trammels, and any discrepancy in this match would indicate movement had occurred. This was one of the items always listed for periodic examination, but throughout one's years of experience with L.N.W. locomotives this was the only occasion when a pair of driving wheels had to be sent to Crewe Works for attention to moved cranks.

When these 0-8-0s were built they entered service with the short length of axle between the crank axle sweeps used as a journal for a third axlebox. A longitudinal frame member, secured to the motion plate at its front end and at the rear to a lateral stay, ran between the sweeps and was gapped at the crank axle. Diminutive horncheeks were fitted front and rear, with a heavy horn stay to secure them beneath the axle. These bearings were removed after only a short time in service, but the longitudinal frame, horncheeks and bottom stay remained until the class were withdrawn at dieselisation.

A memorable event, in my life at least, happened towards the end of the year when the first "Crab" tender to penetrate into South Wales arrived on shed. "Crab" tenders were the 2-6-0 5Fs designed by the ex-L.&Y. C.M.E., George Hughes. Later they replaced the Whale 19″ locomotives at Swansea and proved a great success with enginemen, if only for the fact they were easier to fire and less hungry for coal. Undoubtedly they were heavier on repairs than the 19″ goods, but one came to regard increased repair costs as the inevitable consequence of improved thermal efficiency.

It is claimed the sheer ugliness of these engines won for them the soubriquet "Crab" and the acutely inclined cylinders certainly gave them an ungainly appearance. Nevertheless, they were excellent workhorses and quite capable of out-performing Black Fives under certain conditions, as I was to discover many years later.

One assumes the 2-6-4T engines were nicknamed "Crab tanks" in consequence of their similar wheel arrangement – they certainly didn't resemble George Hughes' locomotives in any other way!

Originally the 2-6-0s were numbered in the 13000 series and this one had run light engine through Central Wales accompanied by a Traffic and a Locomotive Inspector who had a special task to perform. Lead templates had been fitted beneath its cylinders and the Inspectors' job was to take the engine into out-of-the-way sidings and record any places where the lead templates were fouled by an obstruction. Neither Inspector seemed to know the reason for the journey, but after the engine completed its explorations in Swansea we heard that the templates had not been disturbed anywhere over the Central Wales.

When the first Stanier taper boiler 2-6-0 worked down to Swansea one began to understand the purpose behind these cylinder templates. The forty locomotives of this class were the only Stanier type to have cylinders set low down in front, without any degree of inclination to lift them above the line of the driving wheel centres. In many respects they so closely resembled the G.W. 4300 class that many at Swansea shed believed the calumny that he had plundered those drawings on departing from Swindon.

Whether Stanier had any part in the design of the new 2-6-4 tanks which began to appear about this time is uncertain – to me, at least. Conceivably, he could have breathed on their drawings, but if so no mark remained on the finished product. Anything less like the rather exposed footplates of comparable G.W. types is difficult to imagine, since these had totally enclosed cabs unlike any other on a British locomotive before or since. Although everything else remained virtually the same as the Fowler design, enginemen who had to work in them across the Central Wales disliked the new cabs intensely. The 71 miles length of track between Knighton (on the English border) and Pontardulais was, apart from a short stretch at Llandrindod, all single line with crossing loops at most stations where single line block instrument staffs had to be exchanged with signalmen, often whilst the train was in motion. Although a maximum speed of 15 m.p.h. was imposed during the exchange, without reference to a speedometer, drivers' ideas of the rate at which a train was travelling varied wildly. There was a preferred way for the fireman to stand whilst exchanging staffs with a signalman: on a "Crab" tank he normally had one foot on the footplate and the other on the top plate of the cab footsteps, leaning down holding the staff in one hand, with his other hand outstretched to receive the new staff from the signalman. As he had no handhold, he would first turn the small, folding cab door out of the way and wedge his body in the gap. But on these new Crab tanks built with what everyone called "limousine cabs", the doors were great heavy things of steel with a drop-light like that of a carriage entrance door, which could not be folded away to let the fireman wedge his body in the gap.

I certainly heard footplatemen grousing among themselves about this, and assume they complained officially and successfully, for after a time the "limousine" Crab tanks were taken off the Central Wales line. Whether the serious injuries sustained by a Craven Arms fireman had any bearing on this decision must remain unanswered, since one is not sure if it was a limousine cab in his case – certainly he fell from the footplate of a 2-6-4 tank during a staff exchange.

★ ★ ★

A gleaming brand new Black Five moved along the line opposite the platform where I stood with crowds of other passengers on Stafford station waiting for the Shrewsbury train. I was returning from Coventry after a Christmas visit in 1934, and the sight remains clear with me to this day, for it was the first locomotive of that type I'd ever seen – and the first most of my fellow travellers had ever seen, either, if their "Ohs!" and "Ahs!" were anything to judge by.

A Locomotive Inspector had positioned himself in full view on the footplate and his face wore that odd expression of a person who is aware he is the cynosure of all eyes, but is determined not to show it. I recognised him as the Shrewsbury Inspector who had accompanied the 2-6-0 on its lead template mission, and stepped forward to wave. He noticed me and waved back, pointing at the engine. "You'll be able to see her in Swansea!" he called. "I'm bringing her down on the 10 o'clock tomorrow!"

Everyone turned to stare at me – even the pretty young lady with whom I'd travelled in the same compartment from Birmingham, and who had studiously ignored me en route, now looked at me with new interest and the hint of a smile on her face. . . .

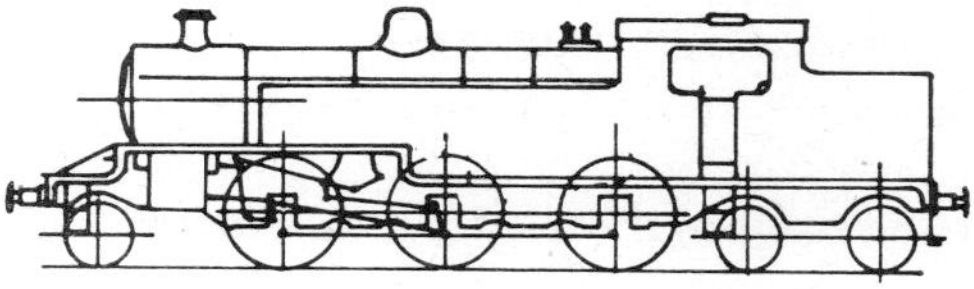

CHAPTER III

Winds of Change

Towards the end of 1933 there had been a stirring of movement in the arcane fastnesses of the Chief Locomotive Superintendent's offices, and the usually effete young men of that organisation had travelled about the land impelled by a new vigour, bringing tidings of tumultuous events that would change the lives of everyone, all because of a miraculous new plan called the "X" Scheme. Prior to this locomotive maintenance had been very haphazard and planning virtually non-existent. Boilers were washed-out only when reported priming, and no attempt was made to co-ordinate other repairs with this wash-out – often a leaking steam joint which needed boiler blow-down would be overlooked, only to have to stop the engine a day or two later. Other parts were repaired as and when they became defective and preventive maintenance was scarcely known, except for specified parts known to have high failure rates.

The "X" Scheme changed all that, and the fundamental ideas behind the plan survived the vicissitudes of Nationalisation to become the standard maintenance procedure for all the Regions, and in a modified form survives today.

The defect reporting procedure had been changed some time before this, and now when finishing with an engine the driver had to complete a "Repairs" or "No Repairs" card – the latter to ensure he had not gone home forgetting to enter repairs. Examining fitters also completed a "Repairs card" if any were found necessary during their daily or weekly examinations.

From the date of the inception of the "X Scheme", locomotive boiler washing was put on a periodic basis – 12 to 16 days was normal, with 24 to 32 days for shunting engines. All other examinations were to be co-ordinated with the boiler washing (or "X day"), and any deferred repairs carried out at the same time. Maintenance Foremen were empowered to defer to "X day" any defect the repair of which would necessitate boiler blow down, or stopping the locomotive for rectification – always providing that such deferment in no way impaired the safety of the locomotive or its crew.

A foolscap-sized "X scheme card" was kept for each engine between 'X days', on which were printed details of certain items needing special attention. However, most of the card was devoted to blank printed lines on which could be written details of deferred repairs and defects discovered by the fitters performing the steam test and mechanical examinations.

The procedure was that when an engine due for "X day" arrived on shed a fitter would carry out a steam test of injectors, ejectors, water gauge frames, carriage warming apparatus, etc., also test smokebox steam pipes with regulator open. A second fitter would carry out a full mechanical examination as soon as the engine was berthed on the wash-out road, and both men would enter defects on the appropriate "X Scheme" card, which was then handed to the "X" scheme fitters.

Equipment such as boiler water injectors, vacuum brake ejectors, boiler water gauge frames and all associated valves and seatings were scheduled for strip-down examination at periods of 3 to 5 weeks or 7 to 9 weeks.

Valves and pistons, slideblocks, big and little ends, were listed for strip-down examination on a mileage basis. Valve and pistons were removed, rings changed and ports cleaned at 30 to 36,000 miles. Strip down or *in situ* examination of big and little ends and side rod bushes was dependent on locomotive type and mileage. On outside cylinder locos it was usually *in situ* at 10–12,000 miles and strip down at 20–24,000. There were variations of this theme, dependent on locomotive type and local conditions. Certain items were looked at every 5–6,000 miles; for example, wheels and tyres were examined and gauged and wear amounts recorded on the appropriate document, but it was intended that both time and mileage period examinations should be done, or at least commenced, at "X" day.

Rigid time disciplines were imposed for blowing steam out of boilers at "X" day and for the boiler cooling-down procedures. Three to four hours, dependent on boiler type, were allotted to blow steam out of boilers before cooling down commenced. Water was then passed into the boiler through a control valve which had orifices of three different sizes. The smallest orifice was used for the first three hours, the intermediate for the next two, and the largest for the final hour.

Similar restrictions were placed on the time taken to raise steam in cold boilers, which varied between 6 and 8 hours, again dependent on type. Of course, these time factors were imposed to avoid the damage which had often occurred previously, due to over-rapid cooling or heating of copper firebox and steel boiler plates, which had different rates of contraction and expansion. Gone now were the days when an urgently required locomotive would be hauled up and down the shed yard in order that the air-pumping action of its pistons could produce a draught in the firebox, thereby raising steam more quickly. Another method had been to use a lengthy stretch of 1″ bore steel piping, U-shaped at the end which slipped inside the chimney, whilst the other end led down to the front buffer plank and was fitted with a normal flexible carriage warming hose pipe, which could be attached to any similarly equipped locomotive. It was then only necessary to open the steam heating valve and a fine old jet of steam would rise from the chimney of the cold locomotive, producing an excellent draught in its firebox. Of course, both methods were irregular, but officialdom must have turned a blind eye to the latter practice because one saw similar home-made pipes laying around at several ex-L.N.W. depots.

To enable the authorities to assess the overall effects of the new "X scheme" it was decided to compare the time spent on running repairs before and after its date of implementation. The thinking was that the running repairs reported by drivers, and fitters carrying out daily or weekly examinations, should be fewer in terms of the man hours needed on repairs after this date than before it. Artisan grades had always to account for their daily 8½ hour work period and also indicate that a repair or inspection had been done by entering their clock card number, and the time spent in the space provided on the repairs card or "X" scheme card.

Before the investigation began, depots were advised that all time spent on "X day" period or mileage inspection and overhaul work must be coded "X", and all time spent on repairs reported by drivers, or by fitters carrying out daily or weekly exams, must be coded "Y".

With a predictable display of pragmatism, the Headquarters circular explained no more than how the required information was to be obtained, and contained no intimation of its purpose, or how it was going to be used. Such a blatant omission inevitably set tongues wagging at depot level, and in no time at all it became obvious to everyone that its purpose must be to compare depot performance. Of course, it wasn't – but this is how it appeared to us: depots which spent the highest proportion of man hours on "Y" repairs would be judged inefficient, since if inspection and remedial work was done properly at "X" days , fewer "Y" repairs would arise. How to avoid this stigma? Simply by booking less time against repairs reported by drivers and examining fitters, and more to "X" scheme work. And that is precisely what happened – instead of the three fitters on running repairs booking 8½ hours each day against repairs reported by drivers, this was reduced by half and the remainder was debited to fictitious work on "X" scheme cards. Nobody at Swansea took into account the possibility that the same idea would occur to staff at other depots, but to my certain knowledge many depots responded in a like manner – probably all who gave the matter any thought reacted in the same way.

Plainly this would result in a distortion of the true position and give a more favourable picture when presented to the Euston hierarchy than was actually the case, but no doubt they were aware of that possibility and had taken it into account. Subsequently events have shown that in the field of planned locomotive maintenance procedure at least, the introduction of the "X" Scheme put the L.M.S.R. in the forefront of world railways.

Investigations had established that a water pressure of 60lb. p.s.i. was necessary to dislodge accumulations of water-soluble mineral sludge in firebox water spaces, which if allowed to remain could lead to serious damage. By the middle of 1934 mains water pressures had been checked at all depots and boost pumps were installed where this was below the desired pressure. The "X" scheme was fully operational throughout the L.M.S. by November of that year, but it had been very costly and the Board of Directors needed to be reassured that the Locomotive Engineers (who often came from the untrustworthy lower classes) were not wasting the shareholders' money. Immediate reassurance was difficult to come by, except to show that locomotive casualties in traffic had fallen slightly in the first six months of the scheme.

However, after twelve months statistics were available which proved the success of the "X" scheme and one has visions of the entire Board of Directors ordering a celebratory dinner for themselves.

Concurrent with the introduction of the "X" scheme, another event of momentous proportions was set in motion, namely the re-organisation of the Locomotive District boundaries. By November 1934 the 57 districts in England and Wales had been reduced to 27 and a proportional cut imposed in Scotland.

James Rowbottom had escaped the consequences of this turmoil by reaching the retirement age of 65, and had been replaced by Thomas Follows, a Midland Railway man who could expect no welcome from the ex-L.N.W. staff at Swansea, who still regarded ex-M.R. men with suspicion. But Mr. Follows (whose brother, J.H. Follows, became Vice-President of the L.M.S.R.) was a man of earthy character, and his friendly approach eventually won the staff to his side.

The L.M.S. had always been split into four Divisions, all geographically similar to the major constituent railway companies:

The Midland Division, incorporating the M.R. and L.T. & S.R. now had eleven districts with its Divisional Headquarters at Derby.

The Western Division, embracing the L.N.W., N. Staffs. & Furness Railways with twelve districts and Divisional Headquarters at Crewe.

The Central Division remained substantially the same as the L. & Y., with four districts whose Headquarters staff occupied Hunt's Bank, a rather grim old office block outside Manchester Victoria station which had been the H.Q. of the L. & Y.R.

The Northern Division comprised the ex-Caledonian, G. & S.W. and Highland Railways, with six districts. H.Q. was in Glasgow.

Each of these new Districts was considerably larger than any they succeeded and presumably the status of the District Superintendents rose accordingly – at least an Assistant was now appointed at each H.Q. depot, but in the main his function was little more than to act as Locomotive Shed Foreman, in charge of the "parent" depot.

A further development was introduced, after a period of settling down to the new district boundaries, with the concept of "Concentration" depots.

As at Swansea, much of the machinery at depots was obsolete and in need of replacement, and it was obvious that outlay on new machines could be kept down if the District "parent" depots only were so equipped where necessary. In future, all major examination and repair work would be concentrated at the parent depot. Such work as valve and piston examinations, hot axles and axlebox overhaul would be performed at these concentration depots which were to be re-tooled, and to have commensurate staff increases. Co-operation with a firm of machine tool manufacturers produced a customised machine, combining a plain turning lathe for axleboxes and other bearings, a shaping machine and a fixed-head drill, all powered from one motor. New gas-fired hearths were installed for white metalling, and "formers" were provided which spelt an end to the practice of pasting white metal – and good riddance too!

Staff was increased to deal with the additional work load at concentration depots by the simple expedient of transferring men from the outlying sheds, whose workload would henceforth decrease. There was no problem here – for the men involved, the alternative was the dole. . . . These denuded places then became officially known as "garage" depots.

Swansea, and all other L.M.S. loco sheds in South and Central Wales, now became "garage" depots in a new District whose H.Q. and concentration depot was to be Shrewsbury – an obvious choice since it was the largest depot, in terms of loco allocations, and the focal point of the lines which radiated from it. "Tommy" Follows was appointed

District Loco Superintendent, but since he had only recently taken up residence in Swansea, he objected to moving to Shrewsbury. Such was his influence he was allowed to remain, and provided with a car to facilitate journeys about his scattered domain.

The new district comprised four former districts:–
Shrewsbury, Craven Arms, Wellington, Knighton, and Hereford.
Swansea (Victoria), Llandovery, Carmarthen, and Builth Road.
Swansea (Upper Bank) Gurnos and Brecon.
Abergavenny, Tredegar, and Blaenavon (15 depots in all.)

The G.W.-L.M.S. joint line ran south from Shrewsbury through Craven Arms and Hereford to Abergavenny Junction, where the ex-L.N.W. line branched west through Abergavenny Brecon Road station along the "heads of the valleys" to Merthyr. In the convoluted layout and complex system of joint ownership and running powers hereabouts was the former Abergavenny district, with sub-depots at Tredegar and Blaenavon.

From Craven Arms the L.N.W. tracks ran through Wales to Swansea Victoria with a Shrewsbury sub-shed at Knighton plus sheds at Builth Road, Llandovery and Carmarthen which had been under Swansea Victoria.

There was also a Midland Railway route to Swansea using the Birmingham New St. tracks to Worcester, then exercising running powers over G.W. metals to Hereford. The Midland reverted to its own tracks from there through the Border country into Wales as far as Three Cocks Junction, then it used the Cambrian Railway line to Brecon, where a few engines were stabled. From there, Midland trains ran over tracks belonging to the Neath & Brecon Railway as far as Ynisygeinon Junction. Some unforeseen circumstances must have forced the parsimonious Midland authorities to lay their own line south from here to Swansea St. Thomas terminus, with another autonomous district H.Q. shed at Swansea Upper Bank, and sub-sheds at Brecon and Gurnos. Gurnos lay on a northern extension of the line from Ynisygeinion Junction, which terminated at Brynamman.

Fitters, fitters' mates, boilermakers and tubers were transferred to Shrewsbury from Abergavenny, Tredegar, Hereford and Upper Bank, but at Swansea Victoria we were fortunate – we lost some work, but regained our losses from another source. The heavy mileage examinations on our large engines went to Shrewsbury, but we retained this work on the smaller types such as the Gadgets, 5′6″ tanks and Cauliflowers, and since Upper Bank was losing a fitter to Shrewsbury, in future we would carry out heavy examinations on their locos (all of which were 0-6-0 tanks).

These decisions resulted from the 120 miles which separated Swansea from Shrewsbury; it was just not possible to run a hot axle that distance without endangering the safety of the line. Nor was it economic to run small locomotives which required heavy mileage examinations to Shrewsbury. They were unsuitable to work any trains, and to run them attached or light engine was too expensive in man hours. The remaining alternative of dismantling motion and coupling rods, loading the parts aboard and sending the engine in a goods train as a wagon also incurred unacceptable cost, and we breathed a sigh of relief when that idea was also rejected.

Up to the time of the Locomotive District re-organisation, we at Swansea Victoria had virtually no contact with Upper Bank, the ex-M.R. shed in Swansea. Indeed, this line had more of a relationship with the G.W. than with the L.M.S. The seventeen miles of line between Swansea St. Thomas station and Brynamman was, I venture to state, the only part of the L.M.S.R. without a connecting freight or passenger service between it and the rest of the Company. After the closure of the line between Ynisygeinon Junction and Brecon, access to it was solely over tracks owned by the former G.W., Rhondda & Swansea Bay, or Swansea Harbour Trust railways. Not only was it singular in that respect, but also in the lucrative freight traffic it handled, and the geography which enabled it to move 750,000 tons of coal per annum so economically; the latter asset it had in common with the G.W.R.

Both these railways operated in coal-rich valleys of South Wales where gradients, falling towards the coal exporting ports, enabled heavily laden coal trains to be hauled without requiring much more than adequate brake power, whilst empty wagons were hauled in the uphill direction.

The traffic on the Midland line was not all coal downhill to the docks for Swansea was, at one time, the centre of the world copper smelting industry, with huge tonnages of ore discharged at the docks annually, much of it transported to the Imperial Smelting Company's works in Llansamlet, over the Midland line.

Many other rare metal ores were smelted in this area, but there was an ecological price to pay for all the foul gases expelled into the air by dozens of uncaring chimneys. Nothing green could grow in the tainted atmosphere of these hillsides, and the landscape around Upper Bank shed and Llansamlet was far less attractive than any pictures one has seen of the moon's surface.

It calls for a stretch of the imagination to envisage two 0-6-0 3F "Jinty" tanks regularly rostered to haul 90 loaded wagons of coal, plus brake van, from Gurnos Junction to Six Pit sidings, near Llansamlet in

Swansea – a journey of only about twelve miles, but with a trailing load of between 1,200–1,300 tons. Yet this certainly did happen at least twice a day, and more often in the mid-1920s when the annual tonnage exceeded 1,000,000 tons.

At Six Pit marshalling yard, these long trains were split into smaller formations before moving on to the Port Tennant exchange yard, where locos of the former Swansea Harbour Trust railway shunted the wagons to the feeder-sidings of the hydraulic coal hoists on the East Dock. The M.R. owned two of these appliances, plus a further two on the King's Dock. Access to the latter coal hoists was over a single line running alongside the east bank of the "New Cut", so called after the Tawe river had been diverted, scores of years earlier, to make way for the new North Dock. The line crossed a busy main road at the east end of a swing bridge spanning the New Cut, and here it converged with another set of metals which crossed the bridge from the direction of the South Dock. Ex-Swansea Harbour Trust 0-6-0 tanks handled these coal wagon trips from the L.M.S. St. Thomas exchange sidings into the King's Docks sidings complex, over a line which had a fairly sharp falling gradient before reaching dock side level. It was inevitable that sooner or later one would get out of control and proceed across the main road at an inordinately high speed – at least fifty miles an hour, claimed several onlookers whose progress over the bridge had been halted by the closing of the crossing gates. This would not have mattered had not a second trip, proceeding from the direction of the swing bridge, attempted to join the converging line at the same time. Undoubtedly, over the years, several heavily loaded coal trips had got out of hand down this gradient, but control had always been regained on the long level stretch of riverside tracks before the sidings were reached. Now, however, havoc resulted, with wagons and their contents scattered far and wide; fortunately, no-one was hurt. Half a dozen wagons loaded with the finest Welsh anthracite leapt off the tracks into the tidal waters of the river, where they lay whilst the tides ebbed and flowed, and all the time their contents dwindled until after a few days no coal remained. It had been carried away by the sea, claimed local inhabitants when questioned by the police. . . .

* * *

After ensuring the organisation of his new district was functioning satisfactorily, Mr Follows turned his attention to less weighty matters, namely the training of apprentices. He called us both into his office, and eyeing us with a critical stare, demanded news of our progress at Tech. Apparently satisfied with our replies, he went on to outline the future training regime he had in store for us. Now we were both turned eighteen, and permitted to work overtime, he considered it useful experience for us to take turns accompanying the breakdown train to derailments. Moreover, he had decided in future we must get used to working on the Midland type locomotives at Upper Bank shed. Although he diplomatically refrained from any derogatory remarks about L.N.W. types, his tone was such I was in no doubt he felt we would be working on the best of all locomotives when we got to this ex-M.R. shed.

The breakdown train at Victoria consisted of two very ancient six-wheel coaches built at Wolverton in 1894, plus a hand-operated six wheel crane capable of lifting a load of 10 tons, and its attendant jib wagon. The axleboxes were packed with wagon grease – a peculiar product of soap-like consistency used then as a lubricant for most wagon axleboxes. As hand-operated cranes went, ours was fairly modern, with a steel jib which could be slewed round by a manually-operated circular rack and pinion arrangement. But this only worked without a load, and if it became necessary to slew with a wagon suspended from the hook, a rope had to be secured to it and all hands, including enginemen, guard and anyone who happened to be standing nearby, would be pressed into service. First we would encourage the load to swing through successively greater arcs, pulling in rhythm with the crane driver's hand signals. Then, when the crane was rocking from side to side, he would call for a final effort and release the slewing brake – round would go the jib with an angry squeal, to deposit its load in the desired spot. It was very nerve-racking to watch, and undoubtedly quite dangerous. Of course, we could only use the crane if we could actually get it to the job. Many a time it was put off the train into some siding or other to allow its axles to cool down, and we would proceed to the derailment with the remaining coaches, rerail the vehicle with jacks and packing and pick up the crane on the way home. So much for grease-packed axleboxes – they really only worked for wagons running at very low speeds.

One of our two coaches was used as a tool van, wherein all our jacks, wooden packing baulks, re-railing ramps, etc., were kept. The other was divided into two compartments: roughly one-third of it was reserved for the man in charge and the remainder for the workers. We were provided with free meals every four hours whilst out on breakdown work. The ration was a tin of corned beef between four, and as many biscuits as one could eat. The mere sight of these biscuits was enough to assuage the most gluttonous appetite – they were a quarter inch thick and three inches in diameter, and they were sweet. It was standard provender for all the breakdown trains and it was served aboard the Upper Bank train, too. Not that we had many opportunities to feast on the "Rock Railway", for the distances that breakdown train had to travel were only short – usually from Upper Bank shed to one of the many sidings along the five mile goods-only line between Upper Bank station junction and Glais Junction.

The former Midland line between Swansea St. Thomas and Upper Bank Junction stations, some 2½ miles in length, was double-track and ran beneath a towering overhang of rock on its east side for some distance after leaving St. Thomas station. It was this feature which evoked the nick-name "Rock Railway", bestowed upon it by fitters from Victoria who travelled by train to Upper Bank after the District re-organisation.

From Upper Bank Station, a single line branched left through Morriston, Clydach and Glais Junction stations. There were several tinplate works and colliery sidings along this line – Morriston Tinplate Works, John Player Tinplate, Graigola Merthyr colliery, and Mond Nickel Works are a few that one recalls.

A goods-only line branched to the right at Upper Bank Junction and rejoined the passenger line at Glais Junction, and from here a single line ran north through Pontardawe, Ynisygeinon Junction and Gurnos, then through Gwys, Cwm Twrych and Cwmllynfell to the terminus station at Brynamman. There was a very smart little two-road loco shed at Gurnos – a scaled down version of Upper Bank, in fact. Its walls and abutments were built in precisely the same style and of the same stone, and it gave one the impression the same builder had constructed both sheds.

There was a sidings complex and a large colliery at Ynisygeinon Junction. Passenger trains via Brecon to Hereford had ceased by the time I joined the Upper Bank breakdown gang, but one occasionally caught sight of a G.W. engine with a few wagons chugging up the steeply graded ex-N. & B.R. line which branched off at Ynisygeinion for Brecon. Footplatemen at Upper Bank were afflicted by severe attacks of nostalgia at the mention of this line and would go into raptures of delight about its scenic splendour. They said that half-way to Brecon there was an incline called "the Bwlch" whose length and gradient made the Sugar Loaf look like a gentle slope. . . .

From the L.M.S. station at Brynamman, a single line ran beneath a road bridge to link with the G.W.R. station. The G.W.R. ran passenger trains from this station via Garnant, Glanamman and Ammanford to Pantyffynnon. From the latter place they ran over the joint L.M.S.-G.W. line to Pontardulais and then over G.W. metals to Llanelly.

Upper Bank shed stood in the V formed by the diverging passenger nd goods lines. It was a building of more substantial appearance than the ex-L.N.W. shed at Victoria, with walls built of stone and a roof that never leaked, although the shed was much smaller, having only two roads. However, facilities for fitting staff were superior to anything at Victoria, where there was no separate accommodation and our upboards, benches and machinery were in the open shed. Upper Bank had a spacious, draught-free shop wherein one could work at a bench without an icy blast of wind whistling round the ears, or rain water dripping down the neck. But having referred to the machinery at Victoria shed as antiquated leaves one no choice but to describe this at Upper Bank as antediluvian. There was a 6″ screw-cutting lathe, which had a heavy flywheel with a handle to turn it – or if no one was available for that purpose, a connecting rod could be coupled to a treadle, whereupon it became a one-man job. The drilling machine was also manually operated with a handle and wheel reminiscent of the type one used to turn on old squeezer-rollers on washing days.

There were still traces of a wall-mounted machine driving shaft ayout in the fitting shop – the brackets still remained on the wall, and obviously a lathe and planing machine would have been necessary at so solated a depot. The removal date of these machines remains a mystery, but it must have been after the amalgamation when the machinery at Victoria became available for Upper Bank locomotives.

A set of manually operated sheerlegs was positioned over a short pit oad outside the shed and, although these gradually fell out of use when he Victoria wheel drop table became available for Upper Bank engines, as an apprentice I used the sheerlegs to lift several 0-6-0 tanks o remove a pair of wheels.

The breakdown train at this depot was even more primitive than that at Victoria, yet it was used far more frequently because the volume of freight traffic was vastly greater than over L.N.W. metals, where long haul freight and passenger traffic to the north predominated. Much of his freight traffic came into the Victoria High Level interchange idings from the G.W.-owned dock complex, and was tripped to the "Beach Sidings" for marshalling – this was where all our north-bound goods trains began. Our originating traffic came chiefly from Berthlwydd and Penlan collieries on the Llanmorlais branch, Gowerton and Grovesend collieries, plus a large tinplate works at Gorseinon. Beyond the latter place there was nothing but sheep and cenery.

Upper Bank's breakdown train consisted of one six-wheel ex-M.R. coach, a two-axle crane with a wooden jib (a lifting capacity of 6 tons) together with an attendant jib wagon. This crane was totally inadequat and after a while it ceased to accompany the train, but the solitary coac always looked rather miserable on its own. It was a miserabl experience to ride in the thing, too, for we had to share ou accommodation with the jacks and packing, pulley blocks, steel bar lengths of rail, cast steel ramps and all the other re-railin paraphernalia.

Personally, I never enjoyed the coffee served in this coach afte hearing about the way scale was cleaned off hot copper plates in th rolling mills which were dotted among the grass-denuded hills aroun the shed. Each morning the smelter works sent their horse-drawn tank round the streets of terraced cottages, paying householders tuppenc per pot for what was known as "lant". As the hot copper plates passe through the rollers, "lant" was chucked over them to remove th scale. . . . No wonder nothing green ever grew in Upper Bank!

The majority of derailments occurred in the intensively used co wagon sidings at Six Pit, on the goods line between Bank and Gla Junctions, but there were also other busy sidings along this line whic we visited frequently. The number of wagons moved hereabouts eac day must have been enormous, but when re-railments happened it wa usually a straight-forward, if rather arduous, task to re-rail them. Neve once, in my experience, was it necessary to call upon the assistance of steam crane to help us with a pile-up.

Quite often the breakdown train was called out to buffer-locke wagons. This sometimes happened during a rough shunt, whe vehicles got out of control and collided violently with stationar wagons in a sidings. The resultant buffing shocks caused the buffe heads of several wagons to leap over and lock behind those of th wagons coupled to them.

Occasionally, two or three wheel sets would have leapt off the rai and would need re-railing, but in the main it was just a matter o knocking out the cotters which held the buffer spindles in thei castings. Then the wagons would be drawn apart, thus pulling th locked buffers out of the castings, and all we had to do then was replac them, and the cotters.

We were called out to St. Thomas sidings about 2 a.m. one Sunda morning just before Christmas. The message described the derailmen as "Several wagons run together on converging roads" and we wer made quite cheerful by the knowledge we would be paid at "doubl time" for Sunday duty – and it would be in our pay tins in time fo Christmas. The breakdown van was already at the sidings when w arrived and the guard met us with the news that it should not take lon

A two-coach train for Pontardulais departing from Swansea (Victoria) station in June 1938 headed by Webb 0-6-2T No. 7807. Victoria had two platforms with an engine release road running between them. Above the far platform the viaduct linking the L.M.S. with the G.W.R. docks complex is just visible.

(Photo: H.C. Casserley)

For no very good reason the Fowler 2-6-4 tanks were nicknamed Crab tanks by most South Wales enginemen. This is No. 42305 at Builth Road (High Level) in June 1951. The steelwork of the bridge over the G.W.R. line between Newbridge-on-Wye and Builth Wells is visible in the foreground. *(Photo: H.C. Casserley)*

Llandovery shed in September 1951. One has a view clear down No. 3 road right through the wall and office demolished by the runaway Super D 0-8-0 mentioned in the text. . . .

The ex-L.N.W.R. shed at Abergavenny, July 1938. Built to house something like 90 or 100 locomotives in busy pre-Grouping days, by this era it conveyed a rather forlorn and empty appearance. *(Photo: H.C. Casserley)*

to clear the accident – a few wagons had run together, causing two of them to tilt sideways, thereby lifting their inner wheels off the line. The outer wheels were still on the rail, and all it needed was two engines to draw the wagons back simultaneously, the guard said, adding that the engine off the breakdown train was to be used as one of them.

Disgruntled at the thought our double time duty would probably be of no more than a few hours' duration, the leading fitter curtly issued orders for the Tilley lamps to be lit and one brought to him at the site, where he and the yard foreman would go to inspect the accident.

I went with him to the foreman's office, picking a way across tracks and around wagons lit only by the odd gas lamp. Oil-lit handlamps were the only means of illumination provided for operating staff and these had a dual purpose, with movable shades of red, white and green, to display signals between ground staff and train crews. The foreman told us that in his opinion the job wouldn't take long to clear once the engines were in position. He picked up his handlamp, leading us to the site to shine its feeble light on the reared-up wagons, and so far as was possible to see, it was obviously no more than a matter of drawing the two wagons carefully apart and they would virtually re-rail themselves.

Then a member of the breakdown gang arrived with a Tilley lamp and the whole scene changed. . . .

Tilley lamps were something new for us in Swansea; prior to their advent we had to use enormous "duck" lamps for lighting our way during night time breakdown operations. They burned oil through a two inch diameter wick and it was almost a full-time job for somebody to replenish their containers during the hours of darkness; if the job was of any size, a couple of dozen would be scattered around the site, each giving off its coils of greasy smoke. From a distance a night time derailment must have looked like a scene from Dante's Inferno. Tilley lamps changed all that, for half a dozen of them would out-shine a hundred duck lamps. They burned an "atomized" jet of paraffin in an incandescent mantle and gave off an intense heat and brilliant light.

Brilliant enough, on this occasion, to illumine the trousered legs of a man, suspended between the wagons. Quite obviously, the poor fellow must be dead, for the upper half of his body had been crushed to a pulp between the vehicles.

"Who is he?" somebody asked. The yard foreman crouched down and the Tilley lamp was tilted to shine on the legs.

"Not one of my men, thank God!" exclaimed the foreman. "This man isn't wearing uniform trousers." We all bent down for a closer look; the trousers looked tattered and dirty and the shoes down at heel, much as a tramp might have worn; in fact, that was the conclusion reached at the inquest, for the man's identity never was discovered. The police thought he might well have been one of those shadowy people who used to creep about railway yards at night, breaking into locked vans in a search for anything worth stealing.

As a result of this delay, the duration of our double time duty was considerably longer than it would have been – but that was money we would have gladly done without.

After listening to stories related by long-serving members of the breakdown gang (such as our jointmaker) concerning really big accidents on the Central Wales line, one rather gained the impression that attending one must be something of a fun occasion. Lots of free beer about, brought from local pubs in cans and paid for by important railway officials anxious to get the line clear quickly, and determined to bolster the flagging spirits of the workers by any means at hand. This is what was said to have happened in 1917, when a whole train of wagons ended up "on the floor" in Llanwrda station. It took two non-stop days and nights for Shrewsbury and Swansea gangs, working from opposite ends of the wreckage, to clear the line. Unlimited amounts of free tobacco, beer and whisky, together with enormous and frequent hot meals of *haute cuisine* quality were the stuff that kept everyone hard at work the entire time, and as the Swansea gang was nearer the supply point and fared better with these free hand-outs, they reached the middle of the wreckage long before Shrewsbury.

I was expecting something like that to happen to me when the next big pile-up occurred at a place called Llangammarch Wells, on the Central Wales line some 45 miles north of Swansea. There were plenty of important officials at the site, but none of them offered to buy me so much as a tuppenny packet of five Woodbines, or half a pint of mild beer – and the Llangammarch Arms was quite close.

When it was all over and we were heading back to Swansea in a near comatose state, I asked our jointmaker why we hadn't had any free handouts. Never at a loss for a crushing reply, he opened his eyes and said, "Because there's no bloody war on, boyo!"

The line at Llanagammarch had been totally blocked by wreckage of the 5/50pm Swansea to Shrewsbury goods train. We were called out about 11/0pm and our breakdown train probably left shortly after midnight, hauled by an 0-6-0 Cauliflower. I was appointed to keep an eye on the axles of our crane en route, and since it was marshalled next to the engine, I suggested the footplate might be the best place to ride for this purpose. Permission was given and we set off for the run to Llangammarch. I had poured liberal amounts of oil on top of the grease in the crane axleboxes before leaving, and taken a full gallon can of oil on the footplate. We stopped at Gowerton, eight miles from Swansea, to pick up the traffic inspector who was to accompany us, and at that stop the axles were just "aired!" The next stop was Pontardulais, only five miles further on, but now the boxes were distinctly warm and despite dosing them with oil, when we stopped at Llandeilo for water the grease in two boxes was literally sizzling with heat, and the crane and jib wagon had to be shunted into a siding to await our return.

The Swansea enginemen were relieved by a Llandovery crew on arrival there. They filled the tank and we left after a stop of only about five or six minutes. As soon as the fireman took the Llandovery-Cynghordy staff from the signalman it became plain even to me that the driver meant to get us to Llangammarch in double-quick time. The load behind the tender was probably less than 50 tons and we fairly galloped up the five miles of 1 in 80 to Cynghordy, where the driver had to make a brake application as we entered the loop for the fireman to exchange staffs with the signalman. Then we ran onto the 4½ miles of 1 in 60 which would take us through Sugar Loaf tunnel, and now the driver really put our Cauliflower to work. It was impossible to distinguish separate exhaust beats, for all that came from the chimney was a continuous roar of noise and a volcanic spouting of sparks that surely must set fire to everything they fell on. When we entered the tunnel they bounced back off its roof into the tender, and one shrank instinctively beneath the short cab roof for protection.

The rest of the run was less exciting, and whilst I rode up Sugar Loaf on footplates on many subsequent occasions, that night-time "thrash" is the one best remembered. . . .

The single line through Llangammarch made it imperative that the breakdown vans should be "run-round" and propelled to the accident from Llanwrtyd Wells, the nearest double-tracked loop where this could be done. When we stopped in the station there, the driver came to advise the Traffic Inspector he would have to return to Llandovery in an hour or so for water.

The Inspector snorted, "No bloody wonder after the way you thrashed up Sugar Loaf!"

"Well, the Rule Book says every effort should be made to clear the line as soon as possible!" the driver retorted. The Inspector muttered some unkind words about mad Llandovery drivers, got out of the van and stamped towards the signalbox.

Our train was propelled the few miles between Llanwrtyd and Llangammarch at a sedate pace, and it was pitch black when successive bangs of rail detonaters, exploded by the passage of our train, told us we were within a few hundred yards of the accident. A little further on the train stopped and we all got out and walked towards the wreckage, laughing and chattering like schoolboys going to a picnic.

It was a mild, moonless summer's night, and in the tiny hamlet of Llangammarch Wells there were no street lamps to light our way – a couple of us carried "duck" lamps which cast a menacing flicker over the vague mountain of wreckage ahead.

Later it was found the accident had been caused by an overheated axle bearing on a four-wheel van, which resulted in the journal breaking off. It had been marshalled tenth from the engine in a train of thirty-six vehicles, and this van together with twenty others in the rear ended up either in a heap on the track, or at the bottom of a 20′ bank on the side of the line. Nobody had been hurt, and the nine undamaged vans had gone forward with the loco, whilst the five runnable wagons and brake van at the rear had been taken to Llandovery.

The only way we could clear the line was to tip everything down the bank, and since we had no crane we had to rely on a lengthy wire hawser carried in the van for this purpose. A stout, single sheave "snatch" block was secured by chains round the trunk of a huge tree which grew half way down the bank, and the hawser reeved through it. The hook at one end was then secured to a likely looking piece of wreckage, and with the other end over the drawbar of the front breakdown van, the driver was signalled to draw back slowly to take up the slack.

One by one, sides or roofs of vans slid down the bank, followed by wheelsets which bounded down to crash through the lineside fence into a field, and we were all quite pleased with our progress by the time our mad Llandovery driver left the scene to get water. Once or twice the Cauliflower had baulked a little when it came to extricating particularly entangled wreckage and it was plain something like an 0-8-0 Super D could well be needed to topple the two or three almost intact vans that lay in the pile of debris.

It was broad daylight by the time he returned with a Llandovery 0-8-4 tank. In the meantime we'd had chance to inspect the wreckage more closely; most of the vans had been loaded with tin ingots which had been scattered far and wide, and sometime later railway police began to arrive on the scene, ferried by special bus from Swansea to guard this valuable metal. We were concerned about our tree, and how it was standing up to this unusual task. An ugly groove had worn in its trunk where the chains passed round it to secure the block and it had a distinct lean in the direction of the line. But it was a mature specimen quite capable of withstanding the loads imposed upon it, and in fact it was still standing in 1960.

The line was clear by late afternoon, but the track had been damaged, and a few more hours passed before the platelayers finished work and the Civil Engineer allowed trains to run over it.

There still remained the problem of loading up the debris. A few vans had rolled down the bank almost intact and it would need a crane of considerably greater capacity than our 10-ton one to retrieve them. The 10-ton lift of our crane was at its minimum jib radius. As the radius increased, the capacity fell until at maximum radius, which would have to be used at Llangammarch, it was only 2 tons. The nearest L.M.S. steam crane was at Crewe, (in those days, Shrewsbury also had a 10-ton hand crane) and so arrangements were made to hire a steam crane from the G.W.R. A couple of weeks later our breakdown train left during the early hours of Sunday to meet the G.W. crane, together with its driver and mate, at Pontardulais. It was marshalled in our train and we left for Llangammarch Wells, where most of the wreckage was loaded into empty wagons. This was a time-consuming process because of the single line layout – as each wagon was loaded it had to be ferried to Llanwrtyd Wells and replaced by an empty one. Although only one train ran in each direction between Swansea and Shrewsbury on Sundays, everything had to be moved back to Llanwrtyd Wells to allow them to pass, and because of these factors the loading-up process lasted for several Sundays.

★ ★ ★

The most demanding incidents, in terms of the physical effort required, were those when locomotives had to be re-railed with hydraulic jacks. We were provided with re-railing ramps – heavy steel castings which fitted over the rail, with a flanged channel each side from ballast to rail level, so designed that a wheel entering this channel would ride up it and be automatically re-railed. Of course, a powerful locomotive was usually needed to haul, or to assist, the derailed locomotive up the sharply inclined channels but it was much easier than jacking it back on the rails. The snag was that derailments usually occurred over points and crossings and we then had to resort to jacking.

The ex-M.R. jacks had a lifting capacity of 20 tons, but they were as much as one man could conveniently carry, and very unreliable. They used water as the hydraulic medium, and there could be no more daunting experience than to shoulder a jack from tool van to derailed vehicle across rails and sleepers on a wet night, only to find it would not work. When in working order, they had a lift of about 14″, roughly twice that of their L.N.W. counterparts kept in the Victoria tool van; they used oil and were considerably lighter but hardly any more reliable.

My first experience of jacking a locomotive back on to the rails happened in Gurnos yard, where a Jinty tank had got all its wheels on the floor, in the middle of trackwork which prevented the use of re-railing ramps.

I was instructed to pack the space between the axlebox underkeeps and the horncheek stays. An assortment of nuts, washers, steel strips and wedges were kept in a special box for this purpose, and whilst the packing could sometimes be inserted from outside, more often it was necessary to crawl under the derailed locomotive, and that was a job for an agile person. This was done to ensure that the wheels lifted as soon as we began jacking up the locomotive frame, and as the wheels would be lifted by the horncheek stays beneath the axlebox underkeeps, it was essential to eliminate the space between them. Unfortunately, there was no way to eliminate the clearance between the underkeep and the axle-journal, and the engine would always be lifted a few inches by the jacks before the wheels followed suit.

The jacks rested on packing baulks positioned on the ballast beneath the buffer plank at the most favourable end of the engine, which would then be lifted until the pair of wheels nearest the jacks were sufficiently clear of the ballast to allow packing baulks, topped by steel plates, to be positioned under them. The loco would be lowered until the wheels rested firmly on the wooden baulks and plates, and they would be secured by scotches driven between the wheel treads and packing.

Jacking would now commence at the opposite end of the locomotive, which would be lifted until the flanges of both pairs of wheels nearest these jacks were clear of the rails; the next operation was to traverse the locomotive sideways until these two wheelsets could be lowered back on the rails.

Now all that remained was to lift the other end of the locomotive and traverse that pair of wheels over the rails. They had been left scotched on steel plates and packing baulks to ensure the opposite end would traverse easily – to have left them buried in the ballast would have made the lateral movement very difficult, if not impossible.

Complete locomotive derailments of this kind were comparatively rare events, which was fortunate for Upper Bank breakdown van carried only one traversing jack, a ponderous thing requiring four strong men to carry it. In common with all jacks of this type, it had a heavy cast steel base in the form of two slides, into which the bottom of the jack fitted. A 2″ diameter square-threaded spindle engaged with a mating nut in the base of the jack, so that when the spindle was rotated manually by a ratchet the 30 ton capacity jack and its load could traverse approximately 2′ from end to end of the slides.

This Upper Bank monstrosity had a lift of only about 6″ which made it easier to use two smaller capacity jacks to lift the loco to the desired height before substituting this traversing jack for the lateral movement.

If the foregoing description gives the impression of a well-organised and systematic procedure, nothing could be further from the truth; complete and utter chaos reigned from start to finish, with everybody losing their tempers and using foul language – especially to Traffic Inspectors who *would* keep asking how long we were going to take. . . .

★ ★ ★

The man in charge of the Upper Bank District moved away after the District re-organisation and his successor was appointed as a Locomotive Shed Foreman, with fitters in charge covering the afternoon and night shifts. Now the depot fitting staff on day turn was reduced to a fitter, a fitter's mate, a boilermaker and tuber.

The classes allocated to this depot were all Johnson 0-6-0 1FT and 0-6-0 3FT or Fowler 0-6-0 3FT tanks. The latter were singular in that they were the only locomotives of that class fitted with the standard L.M.S. V.C.R. gear for working push-and-pull trains between St. Thomas and Brynamman; they were numbered 7477, 7478, 7480, 7481 and 7655. The Upper Bank allocation in 1934 was substantially as follows:

		Built	Driving Wheels	Designer	No. Allocated
0-6-0T 1F	M.R.	1878	4′ 7″	Johnson	7
0-6-0T 3F	M.R.	1899	4′ 7″	Johnson	9
0-6-0T 3F	L.M.S.	1924	4′ 7″	Fowler	5
				Total	21

The 1Fs were confined to shunting duties in the marshalling yards at St. Thomas, Upper Bank, Six Pit and Gurnos; the V.C.R. – fitted 3Fs locos ran the push-and-pull services, and filled in on freight work, whilst the Johnson 3Fs were confined to freight. Although the wheel diameters, cylinder sizes, boiler pressure and tractive effort were identical on both the Johnson and Fowler locomotives, there were several notable details in which they differed: the Johnson types were not fitted with carriage warming apparatus; they were equipped with "dry" rail sanding gear, as against the standard L.M.S. steam ejector sand gear on the Fowler locos. They had round top fireboxes, whilst the Fowler types had Belpaire boilers, and their water tank capacity was some 300 gallons less than the latter.

Upper Bank's allocation of 21 allowed for the six Johnson 3Fs and one 1F needed at Gurnos shed, and there would probably be four spare engines to replace locos in the Main Works, and those at depot undergoing examination, "X" scheme or repair, or "waiting materials" (i.e. awaiting supply of new spare parts, or repair of old parts at main works).

One locomotive would be stopped each week day at Upper Bank for boiler wash-out, "X" scheme and whatever periodic or mileage examinations fell due. In normal circumstances this locomotive would be ready for traffic by 5/0pm the same day, unless the workload was particularly heavy, when it would be held over to the next day for completion. A 10-12,000 mileage examination would require an additional day, or if locomotives happened to be in short supply (as was usually the case) assistance would be requested from Victoria – and our leading fitter always sent one of his apprentices to help out.

On inside cylinder locomotives the big ends had to be dismantled for examination every 10-12,000 miles, which included the usual caliper check for wear. These tank engines had the M.R. type solid forged crankshaft which also had to accommodate the four eccentric sheaves for the Stephenson link valve gear. The width of the sheave bearing areas was quite generous and the feature, together with the width of the big end crank webs and axle journals, had evidently convinced the Derby Drawing Office wizards that the remaining dimensions were insufficient to provide big end bearing areas of adequate proportions. But they believed the width of the big end journal could be effectively increased if they were machined as concave hemispheres, and the big end bearings as matching convex hemispheres.

This idea seemed a reasonable solution but it failed lamentably to take into account the machining difficulties which accompanied this unusual bearing design. Specially shaped tools were provided, but how did one sharpen them, once the edge wore off? There were also difficulties in bedding the brasses by hand after machining that didn't occur with bearings of constant diameter, and these combined to produce that aggravating "clunk" which one frequently heard coming from the big ends of Jinty tanks.

★ ★ ★

About the end of 1934 Black Fives began to appear regularly on Shrewsbury passenger trains. They were built with a vacuum pump beneath the L.H. slide bars, operated from a bracket on the crosshead, and the mere sight of this depressed those of us who had had experience with a similar aberration on our Gadgets. These new Class Fives were allocated to Shrewsbury so it was not really our problem, but everyone at Swansea eyed the vacuum pumps with great suspicion. Then somebody said that Great Western engines had successful vacuum pumps and everyone jeered at him; it was impossible to design a trouble-free vacuum pump, they declared.

Of course it wasn't, as anyone who ever heard a G.W. engine running at low speed will know – there was always that satisfying "clink" of well-designed pump non-return valves to sooth the ear of a locomotive engineer. But we at Swansea remained unconvinced until one day a couple of G.W. 5700 class tanks arrived on shed, after working two excursion trains from Llanelly to Swansea Bay station; we were amazed to discover their pumps would actually keep the brakes off at no more than walking pace! To achieve this result with a L.N.W. pump a speed of at least 20 m.p.h. was required. . . . Nor was it merely the 21 mercury inches of vacuum as used in L.M.S. braking systems – the G.W. insisted on 25 inches, and they'd had no trouble in creating that at about 3 m.p.h. Following this revelation everyone accepted the new Black Five pumps, and began to listen for the definitive G.W. "clink" sound. . . . But it was always more of a rattle than a clink, and after a couple of years the pumps were removed.

There were other design problems with the Stanier locomotives which affected individual items of equipment, but they did not detract from the undoubted overall efficiency of these machines. One thinks of the injector clack box casting mounted on top of the boiler, and the rusty stains beneath it around both sides of so many boilers, caused by steam and hot water leaking from the joints between clack box and injector delivery pipe. At least ten years went by before that problem was solved.

From their introduction, trouble was experienced with the top brake hanger pins on Stanier Black Fives. The brake hanger brackets were riveted to the main frame, which was drilled to accept the pin, and there were flats on opposite sides of the pin head which were designed to prevent rotation when they mated in the appropriately shaped bracket. The pin was prevented from working out by a round, tapered split cotter pin which was hammered through matching tapered holes in pin and bracket, and the split pin legs were then opened.

Even though the travel at the bottom of a brake hanger during brake application probably never exceeded two inches under the worst conditions of brake adjustment, this was sufficient to exert a small rotating moment on the pin – but the flats on the pin head, fitting into mating flats in the bracket were designed to prevent this. . . . Nevertheless, top brake hanger pins began to work out, having sheared neatly through their taper pins, and examining fitters cast a special eye upon them, aware that locomotives coupling rods whirred past those in the driving and trailing brake hangers at enormous speeds.

The only official medium for transmitting information about maintenance problems between management and shop floor was a "Notices" book, into which letters were pasted. The staff concerned signed against the letter once they had read it, and predictably, a missive arrived drawing attention to the need to pay special attention to these pins.

CHAPTER IV

The Outdoor Machinery Department

There was a change in the management of the Shrewsbury district, and the new incumbent proved even more interested in the training of apprentices than his predecessor – if such a thing was possible. In this respect both men were quite unique in that era, for the interest they displayed in apprentice training, and those of us in the Shrewsbury District fared much better than apprentices in most other Locomotive Districts.

Before he left Swansea to take up his new post of D.L.S. at Sheffield, Mr. Follows called us both into his office and, pointing to an array of calipers, steel rulers and steel set squares, etc., spread out on his desk, presented the collection to us as a farewell gift.

The new Superintendent had been cast in a mould of somewhat greater technical refinement than his predecessor. Tom Follows had fought his way up from the ranks, whilst the new man had begun his career as one of Sir Henry Fowler's pupil engineers in Derby Works, and his was the sort of training in which micrometers and slide rules replaced inside and outside calipers.

He interviewed us apprentices during his first visit to Swansea and spoke of his intention to broaden our training by including in it a period with the Outdoor Machinery Engineers section, which in Swansea now came under the aegis of the new District Locomotive Superintendent. In future we were to spend alternate months with the O.D.M. Foreman, whose area of responsibility, one was to discover, spread wide to include such far-flung outposts as electric water-pumping plants at Builth Road, Pontardulais, Gowerton and Gurnos, plus a gas-driven engine water pump plant at Llandovery.

The O.D.M. section was also responsible for the maintenance of equipment such as locomotive turntables, water columns and hydrants, depot machinery and wheel drop equipment, gas lighting and plumbing at Swansea, Upper Bank, Gurnos, Carmarthen, Llandovery and Builth Road loco sheds. There were also six hydraulic coal tips and several cranes on the docks to be kept in working order, and it was the maintenance of the former appliances which demanded by far the largest proportion of man-hours.

O.D.M. Foreman Poultney had under his control as motley an assortment of tradesmen as could be imagined; so diverse and scattered were their duties it was impossible for him to oversee more than a few men each day. Small workshops were located on the South, Prince of Wales and King's Dock, and the staff consisted of five fitters and five mates, a plumber and mate, a blacksmith and striker, a joiner and mate, a gland-packer, two gas fitters – and later, an electrician.

The South Dock workshop was quite close to Victoria shed and had been established to maintain the two coal tips which the L.N.W. owned on this dock; but these served collieries whose seams were already running out, and coal shipments were intermittent. However, it was a different matter on the Prince of Wales and King's Docks, where the four ex-Midland tips were kept at full blast twenty-four hours every day, and we apprentices spent most of our time working on these appliances.

All the machinery was hydraulically operated, by high pressure water piped from impressive central pumping stations on each dock. They all had identical Victorian exteriors, with exuberant facades very reminiscent of Moss's Empire Theatres; whenever one went through their porticoed entrances, one half-expected to hear an orchestra in the background. Usually the visit was to complain about a pressure drop, and the supervisors (all G.W.R. employees) invariably lost interest on hearing we came from an L.M.S. coal tip.

The loaded coal wagons gravitated from each coal tip feeder siding to dockside level, from where they were hauled onto the wagon hoist table by a hydraulic capstan. These were machines which demanded constant attention and since all the mechanism was buried in a pit beneath the capstan head, and needed a crane to lift it out for maintenance, it came as no surprise to discover that the old Upper Bank six-ton breakdown crane was permanently allocated for this duty – and this lift was at the limit of its capacity.

The wagon hoist was lifted some 20 feet to the tipping level by a hydraulic ram acting beneath the hoist table, and at this level a second ram tipped the wagon 45 degrees, whereupon its load emptied through the wagons end door into a movable chute, which then distributed the coal in the vessel's hold.

Incidentally wagon buffer spindles were held in position by a simple flat split cotter whose loss would hardly be noticed in ordinary service, since they were normally under compressive loadings. But a wagon subjected to the indignity of a 45 degree tilt was liable to react by regurgitating any cotterless buffers into the vessel's hold, together with its load of coal.

After tipping the coal at this level, the empty wagon was then drawn off the coal tip by another hydraulic capstan on to an elevated line into the empty wagon sidings, where it was examined by Carriage & Wagon department staff before proceeding to a colliery for its next load. Those minus buffers were "red-labelled" and went onto the "cripple" road to await a replacement buffer.

They were privately-owned wagons in those days, and buffer replacement was a matter for the wagon-repair contracting firms, who had their own staff sited in strategic positions for this purpose.

Forty-odd years later, whilst visiting Garston Dock with the Liverpool Divisional Carriage & Wagon Engineer on an entirely different matter, we came upon two near-identical coal-tips, emptying wagons into rusty old colliers, almost hidden by clouds of coal dust. After I remarked how the sight reminded me of my apprenticeship, he stopped the car and we got out. My companion explained that all the coal loaded here was destined for Irish ports and went on to comment upon the complaints he often received from that source concerning damage to unloading appliances, which was caused by buffer heads buried in the coal.

★ ★ ★

If one needed to get from the Prince of Wales to the King's dock quickly, or in bad weather, it was expedient to hail one of the small sculling boats which plied these docks, usually owned by out-of-work dockers, and for a few coppers a walk of well over a mile could be avoided. En route, one passed a group of derelict ships laid up at buoys in the middle of the Prince of Wales Dock. It was said of these vessels their owners had been unable to meet the Dock charges, and they had passed into the ownership of the Great Western Railway in consequence; if that was so, the G.W.R. must have regretted the acquisition.

The chute of the L.M.S. No. 1 coal tip on the Prince of Wales dock had been under repair, and was left extended over the dock for a few days. It was winter, and when a sou-westerly sprung up one afternoon there was hardly anything between the dock and the Bristol Channel to shield it from the full force of the Atlantic gales. Next morning when we arrived at No. 1 tip we found one of the derelict ships, torn from her moorings by a howling gale, which had then blown this slab-sided old steamer straight across the dock into the lowered chute.

We did not become aware of the full extent of the damage to the coal tip for some time. Rivets had sheared in the chute trunnion brackets anc there was a lot of rust lying about, shaken from the girders by the forc of the impact. But it took Bill Poultney's experienced eye to detect a slight distortion in the very fabric of the coal tip itself.

Derby was advised and a group of structural engineers arrived headed by the Chief O.D.M. Engineer, and in company with thei G.W.R. counterparts, they began their inspection. In the meantime we went about dismantling the coal chute, and it was laid on the quaysid by a G.W. floating crane to await a decision.

How far the damage caused by the ship's midnight rampag influenced the decision of this august body to dismantle the entir structure is unclear; one would not believe a really sound structur would have been more than superficially damaged by such an impact Nevertheless, dismantled it was, and in its place came an "Electric Bel Coal Conveyor".

The chagrin of the Great Western authorities can be imagined! Her was the upstart L.M.S., with only six coal tips amongst scores of simila G.W.-owned appliances in their South Wales docks, up-staging then with an entirely new concept for conveying coal between shore anc ship.

Dockers were asking if this new appliance could ever work as well and load coal as quickly as the old hydraulic tips? Experience provec that when it worked it loaded coal much more quickly, but it brok down so often that over an extended period it was no better – and i certainly cost more to maintain.

* * *

Much of Swansea's coal exports went to ports on the St. Lawrence river which became unnavigable for several weeks during the winter becaus of ice. This meant that heavy work could be carried out on idle coal tip during this period without loss of revenue – but without consideratio for the unfortunate staff who had to work out-doors in winte conditions.

The two coal tips on the King's Dock were in the most expose positions – there was no shelter here from gales blowing from any poin of the compass.

A gang of men arrived from Crewe Works to begin renewing plate and girders whose substance had been devoured by gale-borne sal spray. Among them were platers, riveters, blacksmiths, welders an their assistants, and they set up a veritable workshop with hearths, anvil and little huts, and work benches everywhere. Meanwhile, Bil Poultney and company set about the task of renewing the hydraulic ran which hoisted wagons up to the tipping level. It had become badly scored, spouting jets of pressurised water from its gland each time a wagon was lifted.

First it was disconnected from the table at ground level, and the table lifted clear with our 6-ton hand crane. Then chain-operated pulley blocks were secured high up in the steel work and the carpenter constructed wooden platforms beneath them for us to stand on whilst we hauled the ram out of the bowels of the earth. And, of course, the new ram had then to be positioned in the cylinder.

Not all the work with the O.D.M. department was of such an onerous nature – indeed, some of the jobs we were given were quite pleasant. There were weekly visits to check all the water pumping equipment, water columns and turntables in a district which had the same boundaries as the combined former Victoria and Upper Bank loco districts, and this provided an excellent opportunity to ride on footplates in both directions between Victoria and Builth Road, and St. Thomas and Brynamman.

Together with the O.D.M. foreman and a couple of fitters mates, one spent a week-end at Llandovery, lodging in the house of a platelayer whose wife also provided accommodation for enginemen on "double home" trips during the week. We were there to overhaul the pumping equipment which was situated beneath the water tank on the up platform, and we arrived there just before noon on the Saturday to begin dismantling the single cylinder gas engine and water pumps.

Next day, whilst we changed piston rings, re-ground valves and checked bearing wear, the mates cleaned out the tank and "cement-washed" the cast iron plates – this would dry out before the tank re-filled when pumping began next morning and it was guaranteed to prevent corrosion.

Next day the mates went back to Swansea, whilst we stayed in Llandovery to repair a couple of leaking water hydrant stop valves in the shed. On the Tuesday we caught the 7.45 a.m. train from Swansea at Llandovery, for Builth Road, where we were to renew a leaking loco water column "bag." These bags were fashioned from stout pieces of leather fastened together by copper rivets, and formed into a tubular shape some 12″ or 14″ in diameter and about 10′ or 12′ in length. A brass flange was riveted at one end, which mated to an identical flange on the cast iron water column, and was secured to it with bolts.

Arrangements had been made for the new water bag to be sent from Swansea in the guard's van, and the first thing we did when the train ran into Llandovery station was to ensure it was there. The 7.45 was regarded as the "posh" train from Swansea for it conveyed a through coach to London and a restaurant car to Shrewsbury.

It was also the heaviest passenger train northbound over the Central Wales, and since the introduction of new Shrewsbury Black Fives on the 3/30p.m. Shrewsbury – Swansea (which conveyed the returning restaurant car and through coach from London), and on the 7.45 a.m. Swansea – Shrewsbury, both trains had been increased to seven coaches.

After leaving Llandovery the next stop was Builth Road itself – a nonstop run of 22 miles which was too much for me to resist. Bill Poultney had given me permission to ride on the footplate and now all one needed was the driver's acquiescence. But I had overlooked the fact that this turn was worked by Shrewsbury enginemen, who quite correctly refused to have a total stranger on their footplate.

We had to change the water column bag on the down platform, and these leather bags were heavy enough to need a small rope pulley block, affixed to the top of the column, to hoist them up to the column flange. The renewal work would foul the main line, so permission had to be obtained from the signalman before we could begin. Poultney reckoned we needed about an hour between trains, and this time period presented no difficulty during the day – the line was at its busiest with night freight trains.

L.N.W. pattern locomotive water columns presented a driver with very little margin for mistake when stopping to take water, since they were fixed-head appliances and adjustment for errors in stopping distances were to be found only in the length of the leather bag. Even then, if too much of the bag was allowed to hang outside the loco tank filler, the weight of water in this unsupported length would pull the bag out of the loco tank. This in fact was the chief cause of damage to them.

From Builth Road back to Swansea we caught a train which had left Shrewsbury about midday and would get us to Swansea about 4/15p.m. It was headed by a Swansea "Crab" tank, and also manned by Swansea enginemen who I knew well, so there was no difficulty in getting their permission to ride on the footplate.

These engines were equipped with a Davies & Metcalfe Mark H exhaust injector on the fireman's side, and this one would not work when the regulator was open. Exhaust injectors increased the thermal efficiency of a steam locomotive by utilising some of the steam normally exhausted to atmosphere after its passage through the cylinders, to aid in pre-heating the cold water injected into the boiler. They worked as a normal injector with regulator closed, but with it open a supply of cylinder exhaust steam was carried from the blast pipe by a 4″ diameter pipe to the injector, and this failure to operate with regulator open was one that frequently occurred. It was a comparatively simple defect to remedy with the necessary equipment and spares available, but it is true to say that very often the easy way out was taken: the 1″ pipe leading back to the injector from the steam chest was blanked off, and the expensive Davies & Metcalfe device then operated as a straight-forward live steam injector. Moreover, in service, an injector's failure to utilise its exhaust steam facility could easily go unnoticed.

On this occasion no particular difficulty was caused by the defective injector, for the live steam injector maintained the boiler adequately.

How different in design were the injectors on these new engines from the L.N.W. types! It was said of the latter they had been purchased as a job lot from a firm in Salford, Lancashire, but I always regarded that as a fantasy put about by the Crewe drawing office in L.N.W. days, to disguise the fact that they had been responsible for designing such a dreadful aberration.

The L.N.W. injectors came in two sizes, with 9mm or 11mm diameter cones, but both castings were the same dimensions externally and could only be identified by the cone size stamped upon them. At the loco sheds we never saw the innards of these injectors, since the casting appeared to be in two halves, which were screwed together and the joint firmly soldered round to prevent interference; perhaps the designer believed the sight of its oesophagus too awful for the unaccustomed eye to gaze upon!

Normally, it took about two hours to renew a L.N.W. injector, but it was an uncomfortable task, especially if the engine happened to be in steam, because they were mounted on the firebox under the footplate. 11mm injectors were reserved for the larger boilers on Super Ds etc., whilst the 9mm were for Gadgets and their kind.

One of the causes of injector failure come from defective water sieves inside tanks or tenders, which sometimes eroded and then allowed particles to pass through and block the cones. On L.N.W. engines the entire injector had to be renewed, but on M.R. types the cones could be removed for cleaning. Unfortunately, access to them was by disconnecting the four-bolt steam pipe flange which was cunningly hidden behind the footplate steps. Whenever I had to remove these cones the injector steam valve seemed always to be "blowing through" and the entire job was performed with hot water leaking over one's hands.

It was noticeable that injectors usually failed just as an engine was about to leave the shed to work a train, and then the foremen would stand nearby, casting anxious glances at his watch, whilst we got scalded fingers. On one occasion, we'd done a very quick "injectoscopy" at Upper Bank on a V.C.R. engine, and we were watching it rattle over the junction points at a fair old gallop, with only a few minutes left to get to St. Thomas and work the 11.10a.m. passenger to Brynamman. As it drew level with the junction box it let out a despairing screech from its whistle and came to a grinding halt. The signalman leaned through the window, whilst the driver gesticulated to him, pointing unmistakably back in the direction of the depot. Minutes later the loco was back on shed for repairs to the same injector, which had failed once more. There was no other V.C.R. loco available to replace this one, which meant the 11.10 would have to run as an ordinary passenger train, with a guard provided; of course, one of the purposes of working trains in the "push and pull" mode was to abolish the need for a guard.

The Shed Foreman was infuriated over the driver's refusal to work the train forward with only one injector functioning – he claimed, quite correctly, that one injector was totally inadequate to maintain the boiler with a train of only two coaches. But the long-established attitude of officialdom to a *contretemps* of this nature had always been that in the final analysis the driver was solely responsible.

That afternoon this loco's side tanks were emptied for examination of the water sieves. They were listed for examination every 10-12000 miles, but on this occasion we had to renew the R.H. sieve only a couple of weeks after this examination had been done.

★ ★ ★

I visited Carmarthen shed with Foreman Poultney one day to carry out a repair to some item of O.D.M. equipment.

The shed was quite small, with only two roads, plus a miniscule ashpit and coal wagon siding, but the entire place stands out in the memory for the impression it left of complete cleanliness and tidiness. Not a single piece of coal lay on the ground, and how the staff managed to keep the shed pits so clean must remain a mystery. Even with only three 5′ 6″ tanks to look after, one would expect someone to spill a drop of oil somewhere – but here none was visible. All the other accommodation echoed the same theme – dust-free shelves in the tiny stores, and a mess-room that looked like a parlour.

Although the precise nature of the repair we did remains nebulous, the subsequent reaction of the staff to the mess we must have left behind us is crystal clear – the burly labourer responsible for cleanliness cursed us in Welsh, shook an irate fist in front of our faces, and finally prodded us toward's the foreman's office with his brush. We went inside and stood listening as he poured out a catalogue of our misdeeds in Welsh to the foreman, who sat gravely behind his desk and occasionally "Tut-tutted" in disbelief at such goings on.

When he'd gone, foreman Stimpson reminded us to look suitably chastened when we left his office.

Bernard Stimpson was fitter-in-charge of Carmarthen shed – that is to say he received an additional 6s. a week above a fitter's wage. He'd gone there several years earlier from Shrewsbury, and by now had got the place honed as sharp as a surgeon's scapel. The state of the depot, and the condition of the locomotives and staff morale were unusually good, and this was reflected in his own reputation.

It was not until after Nationalisation that the L.M.S. was forced to accept the staff promotion system which demanded publication of a weekly "Vacancy List", advertising all vacant salaried positions. Prior to that date one was offered a post by letter and to refuse it, for any reason, normally meant one was either sent to the bottom of the league, or transferred from the game altogether. Bernard Stimpson had already turned down two offers of promotion, and kept the letters in a locked drawer of his desk to show any disbeliever; the first had offered him the post of Locomotive Shed Foreman at Moor Row, in Cumberland, and the second a similar job at Bacup in Lancashire.

One had only to visit the Stimpson home to understand his reason for not wishing to leave it. He lived about five miles outside Carmarthen at a place called Ferryside, which had a station on the main G.W. line from London to Fishguard, via Carmarthen, and his delightful little house overlooked the beautiful Afon Tywi estuary. In a tool shed in his garden he kept one of those odd little boats the Welsh made out of strips of osier and tarred canvas, and used for netting salmon in the estuary. They were called coracles, and it took years of experience to master the art of using them.

Stimpson remained at Carmarthen until Nationalisation, when the L.M.S. shed was closed and the engines and staff transferred to the G.W. shed; he was immediately given a salaried position in charge of a depot in northern England. He would have much preferred to end his days at that little place in Ferryside.

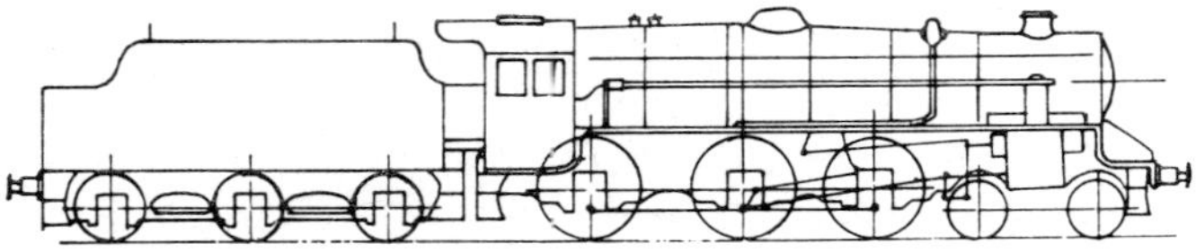

CHAPTER V

Bescot

By now my term of apprenticeship was approaching its end, and about this time a vacancy in the O.D.M. Section at Swansea occurred, and was filled by the senior apprentice. One was pleased that he'd accepted the job, for despite the variety of fine experience the section had provided during training, the prospect of spending any great length of time on this sort of work was not attractive.

Meanwhile, I went around the offices of local shipping agents in a bid to satisfy romantic ideas of encircling the globe as marine engineer, but those visits were of no avail. Then, out of the blue, I was offered a temporary job as fitter at Bescot shed, and later discovered this was to substitute for a fitter who'd suffered serious injury whilst working on the wheel drop.

All I knew about the place was that it lay in the general direction of Birmingham which, via the L.M.S., meant turning right at Shrewsbury and again at Stafford. Stafford was remembered as a good place to live, and since Bescot was only twenty-odd miles further on, one envisaged the place as probably surrounded by the same rural countryside; anesthetised by considerations of this nature, one journeyed forth very much as a lamb to the slaughter. . . .

Upon alighting at Bescot station, the olfactory organ was the first to be assaulted, by the stench of sewage. In that era, it appeared to be the habit of local authorities to dispose of sewage by spreading it over as large an acreage as possible, using a network of small channels for this purpose, each of which had a small watergate to vary the flow as necessary.

Bescot shed stood alongside two such sewage farms run by West Bromwich and Walsall authorities and this situation earned for the place an unenviable and inevitable sobriquet.

Bescot was the parent depot of a district which numbered Bushbury and Monument Lane among its garage depots, and since the former of these provided engines to work Wolverhampton – Euston trains, and the latter the two-hour flyers between New Street and Euston, I walked over the station foot-bridge towards the shed expecting to see a gaggle of Patriots and Jubilees, perhaps even a Scot or two in the shed yard. Instead, the depressing sight of dozens of Super Ds, Gadgets, Cauliflowers and their kind met the eye – or at least, vague outlines suggesting the shape of these types were visible; the entire area was over-hung by a haze.

The clank of buffer contacts, the unmistakable snort of shunting engines and the noise of three-link wagon couplings jerking together seemed to come from almost every direction – as I was to discover, Bescot was really one immense shunting yard.

The shed was not the huge place one expected to see. It had eight pit roads, longer than those at Swansea and by no means as clean. As I walked towards the offices I was struck by the vast numbers of boiler tubes to be seen, old ones lying in heaps in the pits, piles of new tubes neatly arrayed alongside several Super Ds with open smoke-box doors.

I introduced myself to Chief Mechanical Foreman Mulholland, who provided a man to guide me to the lodgings he had found for me with some kindly people in Corporation Street in Walsall. That was the end of a less than perfect day, and the beginning of a period one remembers only vaguely; psychologists tell us the human mind has the fortunate ability to block out memory of its more traumatic experiences!

Next day, as soon as the District Locomotive Superintendent arrived, Mulholland marched me in to see him, and my recollection of the occasion is that I felt very much like an enemy agent being interrogated.

"Where have you served your time?' inquired the D.L.S.

"Swansea," I answered. He was a man with a severe cast in one eye and it had a pronounced tendency to swivel, thus making it very difficult for a stranger to judge his mood; Mulholland, however, knew the eye well and he nudged me.

". . . . sir," I added.

The Superintendent turned to his assistant, who sat at a near-by desk.

"Swansea's in the Shrewsbury district, isn't it?"

"Yes – I visited the place once – it's only a small shed, sir," he replied. The Superintendent turned to Mulholland.

"He won't have had any wheel drop or valve and piston experience – he's not going to be much use to you, Mulholland!"

"I have had experience on valve and piston work – and with hot axles on the wheel drop – and I've lifted engines on sheer legs to get wheels out, sir!" I protested.

I had then to explain the special circumstances which allowed a garage depot to use its wheel drop and carry out heavy mileage examinations, whilst the concept of the Concentration depot functioned as it was meant to in the Bescot District. I should have kept my mouth closed, for that very day I began work on the Bescot wheel drop, removing the driving wheels from a Super D for a reason which was entirely novel to me – to re-bolt loose horncheeks to the main frame.

The shop steward came to me as soon as I left the office that morning, to ask if I would care to join the "suspension fund" at a cost of sixpence per week, which paid ten shillings a day to any man suspended from duty for disciplinary reasons. . . . At first, I thought the fellow was joking, and said so. He soon convinced me it was a serious matter, but I replied I didn't mean to get myself suspended.

"You'll be suspended if you stop here long enough, lad!" the shop steward declared.

I cannot recall if in fact I did contribute to the fund, but the chances are I did, for I am an inveterate joiner of clubs and schemes. However, during my twelve month period at Bescot I managed to avoid official discipline, although several fitters were suspended in that period.

Since then I have made many inquiries amongst contemporary railwaymen, but none to whom I have spoken know of a similar scheme operating at any other locomotive depot.

But what circumstances induced the need for a "suspension fund" amongst fitters at Bescot? Some time before this a casualty reporting system, primarily intended to highlight design faults in troublesome components, began to degenerate into a yard-stick for measuring the maintenance performance of each Locomotive District, by recording the average miles run between locomotive failures in the form of a table comprising all the L.M.S. Locomotive Districts. Ironically, it paid no heed to many factors of prime importance, such as locomotive type and age.

Undoubtedly, for a D.L.S. to find his district at the bottom of this league must have been a harrowing experience, since there was no such thing as relegation to a lower division. His reaction might conceivably have been to gear the severity of punishment, for fitters held responsible for casualties, to the position of his district in the league table. Was Bescot propping up all the other clubs during this period?

★ ★ ★

After removing the driving wheel set from our Super D, we began the job of re-bolting the driving wheel horncheek castings to the main frame. These castings were secured by driving-fit machined countersunk bolts, and if the locomotive had been allowed to work in this condition for any length of time, the bolt holes would have become worn. Then, to reproduce a satisfactory bolt fit, each hole would have to be hand reamered out to the next larger bolt size. These were special countersunk 7/8″ dia. driving fit bolts initially, but if holes needed reamering, bolts with 1″ diameter shanks would have to be fitted.

As the junior fitter I was expected to fill in for any serious staff shortages at the sub-depots in the district, and one recalls these occasions chiefly because on arrival there the jobs one was given seemed often to reflect the distaste of the local fitters to working in smoke-boxes. Nor was I particularly keen on working in them, but as a fitter holding down a temporary job in a district ruled by a disciplinarian, it seemed unwise to complain.

Some time went by before I was allotted a regular fitter's mate, but this finally happened when I was put to work on the "mileage pit" with another fitter, Bill Wilkinson, and his mate. My new mate proved to be an excellent worker, with an inexhaustible supply of unlikely stories about his experiences in the Royal Navy.

A total of six fitters and mates kept the mileage pit going round the clock, with two fitters and mates on each shift. There were some 250 locomotives allocated to sheds in the Bescot district, ranging from Patriots, Jubilees and Compounds, virtually through the entire range of ex-L.N.W. locomotives; they all came on to our mileage pit for the heavy examinations, which included valve and piston overhaul.

From about this period the L.M.S. began a very expensive capital outlay on the provision of water treatment plants in hard water areas – and the Birmingham area was among the first to be dealt with. But at this period locos were still using untreated water, which increased the cost of maintenance enormously – particularly boiler maintenance. It was this feature which accounted for the vast numbers of small boiler tubes I had seen lying around in the shed. There were no less than eight tubers, working in four two-man teams, renewing boiler tubes on a full-time basis at Bescot. A specially designed machine was available to each group for expanding new tubes in both tubeplates, but the tuber's most arduous task was to withdraw the old heavily-scaled tubes from the boiler.

Tubes had to be renewed because the build-up of scale badly impaired their ability to evaporate water, and rendered them liable to implosive failure through overheating. The hard water also affected piston rings on certain locomotive types – on Super Ds, for example, they were programmed for renewal at 10-12,000 miles. This was done by removing the gudgeon pins and cylinder covers, after which, if the crossheads were then pushed forward to their limit of travel up the slide-bars, the piston heads would protrude clear of the cylinders and the piston rings could be changed.

One morning an assistant foreman gave me the task of completing work on a Super D on which the piston rings had just been renewed by night staff. The cylinder covers had to be replaced, the piston cross-head gudgeon pins refitted, and this locomotive could then be fired for work.

On the following morning I found myself on the carpet for not having fitted piston rings in these pistons before replacing the cylinder covers. The assistant foreman, who'd told me the piston rings were fitted, was now off sick and my case remained *sub judice* until he resumed duty. I heard no more about the affair and was content in the thought that no news is good news.

★ ★ ★

Nobody of my acquaintance has ever claimed to enjoy night work, but it is something most railwaymen learn to live with – train crews book on and off at the most inconvenient hours and often a day turn for them means booking on at four o'clock in the morning, and off duty at noon.

Midnight on Sunday was always my worst time, especially at Bescot, where dozens of engines would have been lit up by steamraisers a couple of hours earlier, and by this time their chimneys would be emitting vast clouds of green-grey smoke which filled the shed, to the exclusion of most of the oxygen. Curiously enough, Bill Wilkinson and the two mates seemed quite indifferent to these Sunday midnight gas attacks. Perhaps I might have become had I remained long enough at Bescot. . . .

Control of the activities of staff on the mileage pit was strictly the prerogative of the Chief Mechanical Foreman, and he left written instructions concerning the duties of his two fitters on nights – of course, the night shift assistant foreman was responsible for ensuring we kept our noses to the grindstone. Usually on a Sunday night we would have a completely fresh valve and piston examination to start on – the loco would have arrived, probably from one of the sub-depots, during the week-end.

Bill Wilkinson always worked on the motion parts, dismantling coupling and connecting rods, and then he and his mate would transport these components to the hydraulic press, which was designed to force all the bushes out of the rods, ready for remetalling and reboring by day work staff. Meanwhile my mate and I would remove the cylinder and steam chest covers, "shoot" the piston cones from their sockets in the crossheads, remove the pistons from the cylinders and transport the crossheads to the coppersmith's hearth for remetalling.

Our next job would be to remove the valves. If these were flat slide valves, they would be changed if their thickness was at the minimum laid down. Steam chest ports on engines fitted with flat slide valves tended to wear badly if the valves were not of the "balanced" variety. Gadgets were particularly bad in this respect and one could spend hours bedding new valves to the port bars on those locomotives.

The initial design of piston valve on L.N.W. engines provided a single "ring" some four or five inches wide, on each head, and these were notorious for the vast quantity of steam they allowed to escape to exhaust. These valve heads were already being supplanted by the L.M.S. standard head with six 1/4" wide rings when I started, but I recall removing the occasional set of "wide ring" valves at Bescot.

The carbon build-up in steam passages and on the valves and pistons of locomotives without a facility for steam "atomization" of cylinder oil was often enormous, and frequently caused great difficulty in removing piston valves. Cleaning these carbon deposits from 6-ring valve heads demanded special tools, which fitters made from files ground down to fit neatly in the 1/4" wide ring grooves.

By the time we finished at eight o'clock in the morning, all the coupling and connecting rod bearings and slide blocks would be waiting for the coppersmith, and the work of removing carbon deposit from the valves and pistons would be well under way.

Wilkinson and myself might not work on this particular locomotive again – it was a matter of nicely-balanced judgement on the part of the Foreman to get the best results from this small, specialised group; perhaps he would find it best to have us strip another locomotive on the following night, so that the coppersmith always had a full day's work awaiting him. There were two machinists and one coppersmith on regular daywork at Bescot, and fitters were not allowed anywhere near the lathes or the remetalling hearths.

How different this was from a small shed like Swansea, where we worked right through on valve and piston examinations – remetalled big ends, bushes and slideblocks, then machined and fitted them!

* * *

Negotiations between shopmen's representatives and the railway authorities over paid annual leave had been under way for some time, and eventually it was agreed to award one week's annual leave to shopmen.

Unofficially, one understood that this would entail the employment of additional staff to cover men on leave, and the policy would be, where necessary, to employ extra fitters at the concentration depots, and deploy them at the sub-depots as required during the holiday period. A quick calculation revealed that in the Shrewsbury district approximately 37 fitters and 13 leading fitters, or fitters-in-charge, would absorb 50 man-weeks of annual leave each year. Would this be considered sufficient to warrant the employment of an additional fitter? In the justifiable belief that holiday relief in the Shrewsbury district must be a better proposition than staying at Bescot, as soon as the agreement over holidays was published, I submitted an application asking to be considered for the post of relief fitter there, and received an acknowledgement in due course.

A couple of nail-biting months went by before I received a letter telling me to report to Shrewsbury shed on the following Monday.

On the Friday night Bill Wilkinson, myself and our mates together with a few others had farewell drinks in Walsall. At this time Bill was under threat of a two-day suspension, because of a locomotive failure for which he'd been held responsible, but it didn't seem to bother him that night. Next morning I caught an early train from Walsall station and went on my way rejoicing. . . .

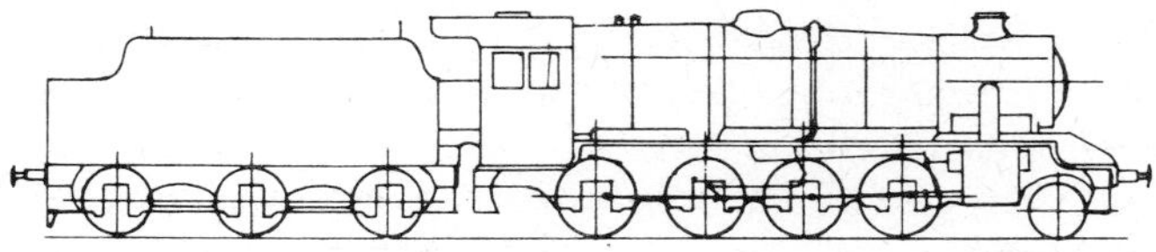

CHAPTER VI
The Salop District

No railwayman ever spoke of Shrewsbury – it was always "Salop". Trains started and finished at Salop and were worked by Salop engines and Salop enginemen, and after a while one became accustomed to this usage.

On arrival at Salop station, I begged a ride on the footplate of an engine which was going to the shed, then found my way to the Chief Mechanical Foreman's office. Swansea's erstwhile machinist, Reg Smith, had held this exalted position with great distinction for some time. He welcomed me cordially, saying he'd already arranged accommodation for me near the shed, and added "....Don't expect any favouritism from me whilst you're working at Salop!" I nodded. "How are you, Mrs Smith.... and Mary?" Mary was his very attractive daughter, whom I'd known as a High School girl in Swansea.
My inquiry was prompted by the thought she would now be eighteen or nineteen. . . . He eyed me with the suspicious expression which often clouds the faces of fathers of nubile young ladies in situations like these. "They're both very well, thanks" he said, guardedly. "But Mary doesn't have much spare time these days. . . ."

* * *

Salop shed was roughly the same size as Bescot, but was situated in a vastly different environment. There was a small marshalling yard nearby called Coleham, where Swansea–bound freight trains were formed, but the shunting done here had not the same clamorous urgency as at Bescot. At Coleham, the shunters seemed to speak in genteel tones, wear carpet slippers and carry rubber covers to slip over wagon buffers before shunting them together. . . .

The L.M.S. and G.W. sheds stood cheek by jowl, some half mile south of the station, but they might just as well have been miles apart for all the communication that passed between them. One always had the feeling that the G.W. men regarded their L.M.S. brethren rather disdainfully – and who could blame them?

"Castles", "Stars", "Halls", all these types were allocated to the G.W. shed, to work their long distance trains to Paddington, Plymouth, Bristol, Penzance and South Wales. There was also a daily rake of dark green S.R. carriages and restaurant car, running in both directions between Shrewsbury and the Southern Railway, and G.W. enginemen worked many trains on double – trips, booking off at Old Oak Common, Newton Abbot, Laira or Cardiff Canton.

All the L.M.S. could show in reply was a handful of Black Fives, Crab 2-6-4 tanks and Prince of Wales 4-6-0s and enginemen who worked trains to Crewe, Liverpool and Manchester. At one time they could boast of working a train to London, but this consisted of parcels vans picked up en route, and didn't last very long. They booked off at Willesden, and returned "as passenger" to Rugby, where they walked to the shed and prepared an engine to work a raft of empty vans back to Salop, mostly over the slow line. Apart from that job, their longest run was over the Central Wales to book off at Swansea Victoria.

The L.M.S. scene was often brightened by the appearance of a Crewe North shed "Lizzie" or "Duchess" on a local passenger train. But the conclusion that they were merely filling – in on these trains between working Anglo – Scottish services proved to be incorrect, as discovered much later. In fact, Crewe North put these engines on Crewe – Salop locals in order to turn them over the triangle formed by the junction of lines just south of Salop station. The turntables on both North and South sheds at Crewe being then too small to turn these 4–6–2 engines.

★ ★ ★

The L.M.S. locomotive maintenance organisation differed from that of the G.W. most fundamentally in the way individual depots were regarded.

Salop G.W. shed was subordinate to Wolverhampton (Stafford Road) only 30 miles distant but, despite its proximity, Salop was equipped with modern machinery to carry out every repair and examination on its own allocation of locomotives. The only occasion they went elsewhere was for programmed overhaul at Main Works.

This feature was common to most G.W. sheds of any reasonable size – they were each entirely responsible for the maintenance of their own locomotives, and every shed was staffed and equipped accordingly. Symptoms of the "Concentration depot" syndrome were never manifest in the Great Western body corporate.

Instead of using the term "District", a cluster of G.W. depots were called a "Division", and its overlord was a Divisional Locomotive and Carriage and Wagon Superintendent, responsible for every wheel that rolled on the railway, with a Locomotive specialist, and a Carriage and Wagon specialist as his assistants. G.W. Divisional Head quarter offices were not part of the parent depot buildings as were the L.M.S. District H.Q. offices; usually the G.W.R. provided divisional office accommodation away from a loco shed, and there was no parent depot in the L.M.S. sense.

The Neath divisional H.Q. office was a rambling old two – storey Victorian house called the "Bungalow", sited on the A474 outside Neath, and these G.W. Superintendents out – ranked their L.M.S. counterparts both in status and salary.

After Nationalism, it became obvious that, whilst fewer in number, some G.W. Divisions were much larger in terms of staff and the number of engines allocated, than any others on British Railways. If memory serves, Newport was the largest with 650, Wolverhampton second with 600 and Neath third with 550 locomotives; all these figures are approximate. The most that other Regions could muster in one district was about 450, and command of these three Western Region districts came to be regarded as the "plum" jobs by aspiring locomotive engineers.

★ ★ ★

The L.M.S. loco superintendent at Salop had obviously set out to make his Concentration depot a model for all to see. To mark the part of the shed reserved for engines under repair, he had a row of bricks dug up between the pit roads across the shed, and the vacant space filled in with white metal. Be it noted this was old white metal, melted off bearings etc., before remetalling took place. The entire area so reserved was kept scrupulously clean, making it almost pleasant to work in the pits.

Next, tins of white and red paint appeared and men started to paint all our cupboards, workbenches and vices in those colours – bench work stopped for a couple of days to allow tha paint to dry. Then it was the turn of the machines to receive their coatings of paint – this time it was a two – tone job in eau – de – nil and apple green. The ancient lathes, shaping machine, wheel lathe and radial drill now looked very smart, even if they produced no better finish.

Large "shadow" boards were erected in this area, with the outline of communal spanners, tools and special equipment painted white on a green background, in order that foremen could easily notice where tools had not been replaced after use, and institute an immediate search for the missing tool plus the offender. It became a mortal sin to leave tools laying about the shed, and this made life easier for all the fitting staff.

The superintendent let it be known he preferred his fitters to wear berets, rather than the more usual peaked cloth caps, but those of us who tried them soon changed back. Peaked cloth caps, although hardly *à la mode,* gave more protection when one's skull came in contact with bits of locomotives whilst working in the pits beneath them.

Although trade apprenticeships usually extended over a five year period, with small increments in wages each year, onedid not become a fully–fledged £3–7s–6d a week fitter for another two years. First one had to be a journeyman at £2–17–6d for the first year, and £3–2s–6d for the second year. Compared with the average working man, one was reasonably affluent: after paying £1–5–0 a week for lodgings and sundry other deductions for Union dues, sick clubs and the like, some £1–7s.–0 remained each week. Why then was I always broke? Of course, I was paying for my new Ariel motor cycle in monthly instalments of thirty shillings – and petrol had just gone up to ten pence a gallon. . . .

I discussed my financial problems during meal hour one night with Bill Cunningham, the assistant mechanical foreman who worked regular night turn. He inquired how much I paid for "digs", and I told him, adding that I wasn't at all pleased with the place for several reasons. but I thought the price quite reasonable. He suggested I should come and lodge with him and his wife, an offer which I gratefully accepted, and of the many digs one had during these pre war years, this was the finest.

★ ★ ★

The first holiday relief vacancy I had to fill was of two weeks' duration at Tredegar shed; after taking his week of annual leave, the local fitter was deputising for a fitter–in–charge on night turn during the second week.

I caught a G.W. local which stopped at all stations between Salop and Abergavenny Junction.There I caught an L.M.S. train to Tredegar – worked by the inevitable L.N.W. 0–6–2 tank. At that same time there were no standard L.M.S. locomotives allocated either to Tredegar, Blaenavon or Abergavenny, and the stud was restricted entirely to ex–L.N.W.R. types.

G.W. northbound passenger trains which stopped at Abergavenny Junction were faced with a fairly severe climb between there and Llanfihangel, and to assist in re–starting heavily loaded trains, special permission was granted for them to be "loose–banked" from the rear for a few hundred yards to the next signalbox. The L.M.S. could provide nothing better than Super Ds for this purpose, and as soon as the passenger train stopped, the points were turned to allow the 0–8–0 to buffer–up to the train.

When the guard signalled right away with his flag, the L.M.S. driver opened his regulator, and as the G.W. driver released the train brakes, the bank engine was expected to shove the train out of the station for some distance before the G.W. locomotive got into its stride. . . . But these trains were normally headed by "Castles", and according to many L.M.S. drivers, what actually happened was that the 0-8-0 would be scarcely halfway along the platform under full blast, before a gap began to open up between the buffers of the rear coach and those of the bank engine!

The ex–L.N.W. line descended sharply, turned west from Abergavenny Junction station and ran past the loco shed. This was the largest in the Salop district, having been designed and built to deal with three or four times the number of locomotives now allocated. During the hey–day of coal as the principal source of power, collieries in Welsh valleys to the west produced a quality of coal greatly in demand for use in marine boilers and much of it was worked to northern ports by Abergavenny engines and men. Famous among these long distance coal trains were those which conveyed coal for shipment to Scapa Flow, the Grand Fleet's base during the 1914/18 war.

In 1938, with a locomotive allocation of only 35 or 40, the interior of Abergavenny shed often had a distinctly unused appearance, when the usual weekday ten or twelve locos were scattered about in a shed built to house fifty or sixty.

The place had a couple of unusual features that were indicative of its former importance as a predominantly freight–orientated shed: on certain L.N.W. locos with unbalanced slide valves the steam chest ports wore badly in predictable areas, and often needed main works attention. Although it was no longer in use, Abergavenny had been equipped with a milling machine, driven from overhead shafting, which had cutters designed to re-surface the steam chest port surfaces of locomotives fitted with slide valves.

The wheel drop must have been one of the very first ever installed by the L.N.W. for it was quite primitive, having a flat table without a pit, and had been designed to remove only the small diameter wheels of freight engines. From the end of the wheel drop road, small turntables, and grooves in the floor bricks enabled staff to push a wheel set under an overhead gantry pulley block for positioning in the lathe for tyre or journal turning.

Abergavenny provided a couple of Super Ds and Gadgets to work at Blaenavon shed, which was on a line that branched off the Abergavenny–Merthyr route at Brynmawr. A fitter–in–charge looked after this depot, carrying out minor repairs and brake adjustments, but

Abergavenny fitters claimed relieving this man was their prerogative and I was not allowed anywhere near the place. Only once did I visit Blaenavon, and then only for a few hours to assist with a repair that needed two fitters

* * *

The train from Abergavenny ran to Merthyr, but I changed for Tredegar at Nantybwch, with only Sirhowy station between there and my destination. This line continued south through the Sirhowy Valley to Newport (Mon), where fussy little L.N.W. Gadgets hauled their trains in and out of the G.W. station alongside the "Castles" which were working the expresses between South Wales and Paddington.

By some devious means, the obtrusive L.N.W. even managed to obtain access to the docks in Newport, where there was a small yard called "London North Western Sidings".

The Tredegar foreman had found digs for me with a dear old lady who lived alone in a tiny "two–up and two–down" cottage in Mafeking Terrace. All the cottages on that side of the terrace cowered beneath the threatening bulk of a mountain, and their back yards were unfenced, without a readily definable boundary between them and the mountains beyond, where roamed the feral Welsh sheep. Only the two rooms downstairs had any gaslight, and that night I retired to my back bed–room with a candle. Sometime during the night I was awakened by a noise, and opened my eyes to the stygian blackness of the room, then realised I could not light my stub of candle, since I had left my matches downstairs. The noise came again, seemingly from the back yard, so I got out of bed and groped my way to the windows. At first there was nothing to see. . . . then a lighter, indistinct shape moved outside – it seemed much larger than a dog. Then others appeared and suddenly there was the unmistakable clatter of a dustbin lid falling onto the ground. . . .

The mountain sheep were making their nightly foray on Mafeking Terrace's dustbins !

* * *

On my first full day at Tredegar I observed a fairly lengthy train of work–worn non–corridor stock, hauled by an 0–8–4 tank, drawing to a halt a couple of hundred yards from the shed. What made this stop noticeable was the absence of any fixed signals at danger, or a station; that was a full mile further along the line.

For a moment the thought crossed my mind that the loco had failed, then the loco gave a few short pops of its whistle and, as if by magic, dozens of coach doors opened and hundreds of coal–begrimed miners got out. They banged the doors shut and climbed the lineside fence, obviously heading towards the streets of terraced houses beyond. The guard waved his green flag and off went the train to the station, where I watched it disgorge a few dozen remaining miners.

Apparently this was customary practice, repeated by other trains that carried miners home at the end of each shift.

I had my first experience of a fractured coupling rod crank pin on a Super D whilst at Tredegar , and in fact that was the only happening of any consequence during my sojourns there.

Normally, each week day was the same as the next: there were daily examinations of passenger train engines, and weekly examinations of freight engines to perform, as well as attention to be given to any necessary repairs or adjustments one discovered. As engines came to the shed and drivers filled in repair cards for them, one collected these from the shed foreman's office and either rectified the defects, or deferred them to "X" scheme day; the latter action could only be taken with the agreement of the foreman.

Brake adjustments, small steam valve gland leaking, steam pipe flanges leaking, brake blocks renewing, or even the occasional piston packing blowing – those were the sort of things one dealt with routinely.

A broken crank pin was an eventful happening at a shed like Tredegar. It occurred at Nantybwch station, and we were conveyed there by a special light engine, together with the foreman and a couple of helpers.

When first built, the coupled wheels of these 0–8–0s were linked together by three independent coupling rods each side. The crank pins of most eight–wheel coupled engines are connected by a single coupling rod each side, with two gradient (or junction) pins providing for the necessary vertical movement between first and second, and third and fourth wheel sets. On L.N.W. 0–8–0s, the same provision for vertical movement was by three short rods coupling the first wheelset to the second, the second wheelset to the third, and the third to the fourth. It will be seen that the crankpins of the second and third wheelsets had each to be long enough to provide bearing area for the bushes of two coupling rods, and these were the crankpins most susceptible to fracture, for obvious reasons. The second pair of wheels were the driving wheels, and it was these coupling rod crankpins that usually broke off.

Crankpin failures became more frequent as this class got older, until the increasing number of breakages forced the C.M.E. into a modification of the entire fleet, which entailed fitting shorter crankpins in the driving and intermediate wheelsets, and the provision of a normal coupling rod with two gradient pins.

★ ★ ★

I spent a few weeks at Abergavenny during the summer of 1938, lodging in the home of one of the fitters mates at the shed. In this mountainous terrain, where gradients of 1 in 60 were common place, and short stretches of 1 in 40 by no means rare, the efficiency of rail–sanding equipment was of prime importance.

When enginemen booked on at Abergavenny, or Tredegar, to prepare an engine for duty, the first thing they did was to ensure that the sand valves were working. Sand often became damp for no apparent reason in the boxes, and this was the usual cause of their failure to operate. Even if the sand was dry, and running down the pipes, in a strong cross wind there was a good chance of it being blown off course in the two or three inches between the sand pipe end and the rail.

L.N.W. "Claughtons" and "Princes" sand pipes were actually fitted with a wind shield to counter this, but these had to be so close to the rail they were often broken off.

All important, in the design and lay–out of sanding gear, was the need to protect the sand boxes from moisture ingress. The L.N.W. achieved this objective with front sand valves, but were less successful with those provided for the reverse direction. Those on Super Ds had the filler pipe lids mounted on the raised footplate floor under the driver's and fireman's seats, and were prone to water getting in as a result.

Strangely, enginemen never seemed quite so concerned over defective back sands on these locos as they were about those for the foreward direction. One wonders if that was because they had given up hope of them ever working, or the discovery they weren't quite so necessary tender–first, when the tender wheels had a cleaning action on the rails.

In this district Super Ds worked as many trains tender–first as in the other direction, and about this time several of the class, allocated to both Abergavenny and Tredegar, began to appear fresh from shops with a smart new back cab, built on the tender to give protection during tenderfirst working. And they were also fitted with the new L.M.S. steam sand valves on the trailing coupled wheels, designed to squirt steam–borne sand precisely into the tangential point of wheel / rail contact, as the loco went astern.

This steam sanding apparatus became standard on B.R. steam locomotives, with only one rather disastrous, albeit well–intentioned, modification on a few engines: the copper pipe, which carried steam to the ejector at the bottom of the sand pipe, was diverted into the sand box and formed a coil. The heat so generated should be sufficient to keep the sand dry, or dry out any damp sand put in inadvertently.

Drying sand for locomotive use was always an expensive business, and up to the mid–1930s it had been dried in enormous furnaces which had grates of locomotive proportions, even using a complete set of loco firebars.

Then a firm specialising in railway products introduced their Kelbus Sand Dryer, with a much reduced appetite for coal, and far more compact. So productive were they that the one installed at Swansea could keep the entire Salop District supplied with dry sand, and it was the ideal place to site one for this purpose for train loads of sand were shovelled off nearby tracks every winter when gales blew. . . .

One man kept it going – shovelling wet sand from the wagons into the Kelbus hopper, filling tarpaulin bags with dry sand, loading them into vans destined to depots throughout the district on a regular basis, each shed having its own weekly quota of dry sand. . . . The job lasted for some months before the truth became apparent: when unloaded into storage hoppers at the various depots most of the bags were found to contain damp sand. The sand was composed of grains of such miniscule size that its consistency was flour–like, and the drying–out process introduced a degree of dehydration which enabled it to absorb moisture even from a humid atmosphere. The B.R. steam coil succeeded in its purpose, but it conferred upon the sand an unfortunate ability to transform itself into a homogenous block, so hard it had to be chipped out of the sand boxes with bars.

Sands of larger grain size apparently had a marketable value for commercial use, and a really satisfactory material did not come to hand until the 1960s, when a waste product from the foundries of British Steel was purchased for diesel locomotive sandboxes.

* * *

During a few weeks at Swansea Victoria and Upper Bank on holiday relief that summer, I learned that a vacancy for a fitter at Victoria had occurred and promptly applied to fill the job. There were no other applicants and a few weeks later I was officially transferred back to Swansea, receiving an extra shilling in my pay tin each week as a result. This came about because all the Railway Companies held the extraordinary belief it was cheaper to live in what they considered a rural town, like Shrewsbury, than in an industrial one like Swansea. The weekly rate for a fitter in Shrewsbury was 67/6d, and in Swansea

68/6d, so I said a regretful goodbye to Bill Cunningham and his wife, and set off to Swansea on my motor bike. . . .

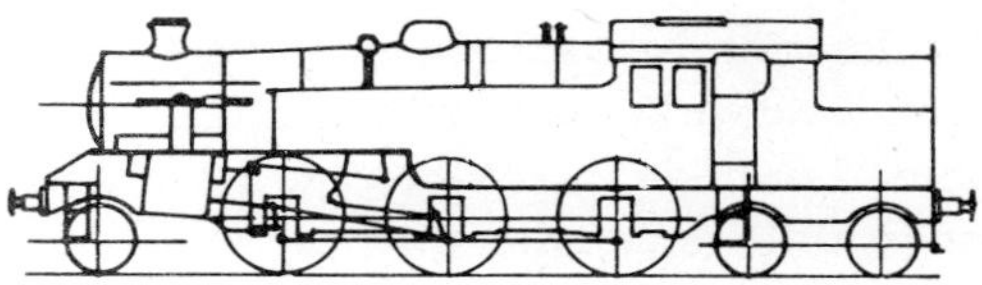

CHAPTER VII
The Lancashire & Yorkshire Railway

Sir William Stanier's fine 8F 2–8–0s started to appear regularly on freights over the Central Wales shortly after I returned to Swansea. Enginemen had nothing but praise for them, after several decades of experience with Super Ds on these trains.

Little else had changed much at Swansea during my absence, but things were not going to remain that way for long.

Several weeks before the declaration of War, we had received drawings from Derby illustrating the method of fastening "anti–glare" sheets to the cabs and tenders of locomotives allocated to Swansea. These were intended to shroud the glare of open firebox doors from night–flying aircraft and mainly involved the removal of certain rivets or bolts from the cab roof and tender front and replacing these with hook–bolts. Tarpaulin sheets were to be stretched between these bolts and tensioned with rubber loops, or light coil springs. By the time the kits arrived, all our locomotives had been fitted with hook bolts and the job of positioning the "anti–glare" sheets was comparatively simple.

About this time I was sent to act as fitter–in–charge at Gurnos for a few weeks and so missed the most serious derailment ever to occur on the Central Wales line. A Shrewbury – Swansea freight, headed by a Super D, got out of control after leaving Sugar Loaf Halt, where it had (or should have) stopped to pin down brakes. This train ran through the single line tunnel and got out of control on the 4½ miles of 1 in 60 down to Cynghordy single–line, so the signalman at Cynghordy had no alternative but to turn the runaway into the sand–drag.

The locomotive demolished an enormous buffer stop, ploughed on into a field and rolled onto its side, whilst the wagons spewed their loads everywhere as they leapt one on top of the other in a fine old pile–up.

The loco was manned by Salop men and the fireman survived the injuries he sustained when leaping off the footplate as the train hurtled through Cynghordy station. The driver stayed on the footplate and received injuries from which he died a few days later in Llandrindod hospital, where both men had been taken after the accident.

Swansea breakdown train was sent to the accident, but on arrival there was little they could do without a steam crane. The freight had consisted of some 25 wagons and brake van, the majority of which had jumped enthusiastically onto the pile of wreckage, whilst of the remainder, a couple had been derailed and a few, including the brake van, still stood on the rails of the sand drag. Remarkably, because of the length of the sand drag, the main line was never blocked by this accident.

On a Sunday, a couple of weeks later, Crewe and Rugby steam cranes arrived to re–rail the 0–8–0 and its tender plus those of the wagons which were in a fit state to run on their own wheels – the remainder being loaded on to low wagons. The tender was too badly damaged to travel to Crewe Works on its own wheels and was taken to Llandovery for loading on to a Weltrol wagon.

I finished my relief at Gurnos in time to be awarded the job of dismantling the motion and coupling rods of the damaged loco at Llandovery, to enable it to be hauled dead to Crewe Works, with the Weltrol attached to the loco's intermediate drawgear. The loco wheels had to be gauged to ensure that no distortion of the axles had occurred during derailment, and also that the tyres had not moved on the wheel centres. During this examination one could not fail to notice the enormous "flats" worn into the tyre treads. These were approximately 4″ long, and had obviously been caused by the locomotive skidding with locked wheels for a comsiderable distance – yet there were not matching flats to be found on the tender wheels, when I examined these out of curiosity.

I doubted if the loco was really fit to travel dead to Crewe with these flats, but the Swansea shed foreman had seen them and was quite happy to allow it to make the journey. He gave me the job of accompanying the special train which hauled the locomotive and Weltrol to Crewe Works.

I rode on the footplate of the dead engine for the first part of the journey and was quite surprised to discover how rough a locomotive became when the wheels got out of step once the coupling rods were removed. The flats on the wheel treads caused severe vibration, adding to the general clatter and noise. It was mid–winter, and without a fire under the boiler the footplate became bitterly cold. When we stopped at Llandrindod for water, I abandoned the footplate for the cosy warmth of the guard's brake van, and only left it for a quick inspection of the dead engine at each stop.

★ ★ ★

One of the big 0-8-4 7F tanks sandwiched between two G.W.R. locomotives at Abergavenny in 1938. The dreadful aberration of dual-purpose reversing gear is not visible but the axlebox mechanical lubricator can be seen mounted above the first and second pair of wheels.

Webb 1P 2-4-2T No. 46601 heading a Dunstable-Leighton Buzzard train into Leighton station, May 1945. The two-road engine shed is seen behind the rear coach; this view gives little impression of the curvature and incline of the branch line as it climbed up to the main line from Wing Level Crossing. (Photo: H.C. Casserley)

Various stages of lifting an ex-L.N.W.R. Super D back on to the rails after a bad derailment (precise date unknown) near Cynghordy.

Swansea was attacked by the Luftwaffe several times, most heavily during a three–night blitz in September 1940. A stick of bombs fell across the shed yard and a couple of engines were slightly damaged. Black Five 5050 was one of these, but she managed to work a Salop train next morning and got away just in time; about midday, unexploded bombs were found among the sand dunes between Swansea Bay and Mumbles Road stations and the line was closed for eight hours whilst these were dealt with.

Due to changing traffic conditions, locomotive hours "in use" were now going up considerably – a feature which was reflected in the increased demands being made upon depot maintenance facilities and it became necessary for Fitting staff grades to work overtime to cope with this increased work load. An almost inevitable consequence of the sustained high piston loadings now being imposed on locomotives began to manifest itself in older locomotives (such as L.N.W. Super Ds) in the shape of main frame fractures. Towards the end of the war there was also an increase in these fractures amongst the more modern locomotives.

At Swansea the fitting staff worked overtime on a day–to–day basis: one might be called upon to work an extra three, four or even five hours two or three nights each week, together with an occasional Saturday afternoon or Sunday duty. But the staff at some depots had managed to negotiate overtime on a rostered basis, as I discovered when I transferred to the ex–Lancashire & Yorkshire Railway shed in Bolton at the beginning of 1941.

After several months of fruitless search for a house in Swansea, my fiancée and I had postponed our marriage until suitable accommodation could be found. Then, having been offered a small house in a village called Little Hulton, near Worsley in Lancashire, we took out a map and discovered a number of L.M.S. locomotive sheds within reasonable travelling distance.

Patricroft, serving Manchester Exchange station on the L.N.W. route between Liverpool and Leeds, was the nearest large shed, and Little Hulton station stood on the line which branched off the Liverpool to Leeds route at Eccles. Patricroft shed was close to Eccles station – indeed, it was sited in the V of this junction and there were only Monton Green, Worsley and Walkden Low Level stations between there and Little Hulton. Along this line, in the opposite direction, the next station was Plodder Lane, where there was a rather small L.N.W. shed which served the Bolton Great Moor Street terminus, some two miles further on.

In the belief one stood a better chance of transfer to a large shed like

Patricroft, in my letter I mentioned this as first choice and Plodder Lane as an alternative. The reply regretted there were no vacancies at either depot, but I could be accommodated at Bolton Burnden shed.

This L.& Y shed at Bolton was considerably larger than Swansea Victoria. The total area covered by the shed building and yard was also greater than those of Salop or Bescot, yet the number of locomotives allocated was considerably less. However, all the locomotives turned off Horwich Works after overhaul (and those newly built), came to Bolton for a few days running–in before proceeding to the home depot. The boilers of certain fresh–off locos were washed out on arrival, but this depended on the type of overhaul the boilers had received.

There would usually be some half dozen fresh–offs working trains specially rostered for this purpose, and these effectively increased the number of turns allocated to the depot.

The decision of the L.M.S. Board to install standard types of mechanical coaling plants at certain depots must have been governed by such factors as the annual tonnage supplied, and the daily number of locomotives requiring coal. Bolton shed had evidently met at least one of these requirements, for a mechanical plant had been erected there before the outbreak of war.

Scores of passenger trains to and from Bolton Trinity Street station, were worked by those great little L.&.Y. 2–4–2 Radial tank engines and most of this class had very small capacity coal bunkers which needed frequent replenishment, resulting in a near continual stream of these locos on and off Burnden shed every day. Most were "foreigners" from sheds like Blackpool, Bank Hall, Fleetwood etc. and, except for those needing repair, we fitters saw their coming and going only from a distance.

The shed building had the finest fitting shop I had ever seen. At one end there was a separate tool room and on the adjoining fitting shop wall stood a blacksmith's hearth, around which were the cupboards and workbenches for the two boilermakers and their mates, the tubers. The rest of the shop was devoted to machinery, enormous workbenches, and cupboard space for the fitters and mates – plus a tiny office for leading fitter Leonard Taylor. Compared with the ex.L.N.W. depots of my acquaintance, this place was paradise.

There were two lathes and a radial drill, all driven from overhead shafting, but noticeably absent was a shaping machine for planing axleboxes and crossheads, or a hearth for re–metalling these components. Every component needing that treatment had to be sent to the "concentration" depot at Newton Heath, north of Manchester.

In addition to the boilermakers, there were seven fitters, two Grade 3 fitters, two apprentice fitters and five fitters' mates at Bolton. In 1941 the locomotive allocation at Bolton was substantially as follows :

		Original Coy.	Build Date	Driving Wheels	Designers	No. Allocated
0-6-0ST	2F	L. & Y.	1891	4′6″	Aspinall	5
2-4-2T	2P	L. & Y.	1889	5′8″	Aspinall	9
2-4-2T	3P	L. & Y.	1898	5′8″	Asp./Hughes	6
0-6-0	3F	L. & Y.	1889	5′1″	Aspinall	8
0-6-0	3F	L. & Y.	1909	5′1″	Hughes	4
0-8-0	7F	L.M.S.	1926	4′8½″	Fowler	5
2-6-4T	4P	L.M.S.	1935	5′9″	Stanier	9
					Total	46

In addition to the above, at Bolton we maintained three rail motors, Nos. 10600, 10606 and 10616. These had outside cylinders, Walschaerts valve gear, steam chests with balanced slide valves above the cylinders, and a coal bunker inside the cab. Behind the cab, the loco main frame was extended to form a pivotal bearing whereon one end of the 50′ coach body rested – a normal bogie supporting the opposite end.

These operated passenger services between Blackrod and Horwich and one recalls the coach interiors as quite singular, for the seats were covered in closely woven wicker work. The coaches were also fitted with retractable vacuum operated entrance steps mounted both sides, at the middle and ends of the body. The trailing coupled wheels of these little engines were the driving wheels, which also carried the weight of one end of the coach, and the axlebox bearings were prone to overheating in consequence.

The wheel drop at Bolton was not used as often as that at Swansea, and it lay idle for weeks on end. I saw it used on several occasions to remove the water pick–up gear trunk legs of 2–4–2 Radial tanks, which were vacuum operated and designed to take water from troughs in both directions of travel. When the troughs froze over during winter, the impact of the water scoop in the ice was sometimes sufficient to fracture the vee–shaped cast iron water trunking, and the easiest way to dismantle and renew this hefty casting was to lift and lower it on the wheel drop table.

After leaving Stafford, the only time I ever got near enough to touch a "Claughton" was whilst working a night shift at Bolton during the winter of 1942. I was astonished to see one of them on the wheeldrop road minus a driving wheel set, for I really believed they had all been cut up, but in fact I learned a few were still running. This one was No.6006, and she had apparently run a leading coupled axle hot – and that, of course, was the driving wheelset with a marvellous crank shaft to which all four pistons were coupled.

The only time I used the wheel drop was to change an occasional engine spring on night shift, but I watched the process of removing the trailing wheels of the four–coupled rail motor engines with interest. The coach body was jacked up until it was clear of the engine frame. Then the 0–4–0 was positioned over the wheel drop and the rear of its frame also had to be supported before the trailing wheelset could be lowered down the wheel drop well. A special four wheel trolley was run under the frame and the jacks were released until the rear end of the engine rested upon it, and it could then be run off the wheel drop.

★ ★ ★

All heavy repairs and examinations on Bolton locos were carried out at Newton Heath concentration depot, Bolton being "garage" depot in the intended sense of the word. However, it was a busy place, with more foreign engines calling each day than at many a shed twice its size; to a loco man, of course, any engine not allocated to his depot was a "foreigner".

This large daily flow of engines inevitably led to an increase in running repairs, since foreign drivers, rostered to take their engine to shed for coal, would often find a minor repair to report on arrival. As a result, at a shed of comparable allocation like Swansea, only three fitters were needed to look after running repairs each day, but at Bolton this work required four, and often five, fitters. One of the factors which increased our work load on night shift were the fifteen engines which left the shed between 5 and 8 o'clock every morning to work passenger trains; each needed a daily examination to ensure its fitness to haul such trains, and a fitter would need up to 30 minutes to examine each passenger engine.

Drivers here didn't seem to attach as much importance to the function of sand valves as their comrades in South Wales, no doubt because they were not confronted by such mountainous terrain. But they had other idiosyncrasies, particularly with regard to the Gresham and Craven Patent Automatic Restarting injectors, with which all L.& Y. locomotives were equipped.

These things were studded straight on to the fire– box, which meant the steam had to be blown out of the boiler before the injector could be changed – and changing these injectors was a favourite pastime at most ex–L.& Y. sheds. The injector clack was badly designed, with a coned seating only about 1¼″ in diameter which often leaked steam through the injector body and heated the water in the feed pipe, thereby causing a vapour lock that prevented the injector from working.

There was a stop valve to isolate the clack and it could be re–faced with steam in the boiler, but there was no similar facility to isolate a leaking steam valve, which could also cause the feed water pipe to overheat. The only way enginemen could get rid of the vapour lock was by bathing the footplate section of feed water pipe with cold water. As if to anticipate this need, L.& Y. tenders were fitted with a footplate water tap, and of course, each engine carried a water bucket. . . .

One has a hazy recollection of seeing ex–L.& Y. 4–6–4 passenger tanks rattling past the shed on the Manchester line with passenger trains. I certainly never saw one on Bolton shed and could have confused them with glimpses of their look–alike relatives, the George Hughes 4–6–0 tender engines. Apparently, they were identical in every other respect and the Bolton fitters claimed the tank version was the heaviest passenger tank ever to work in the british Isles. The 4–6–0s came on to the shed only rarely, and I got the impression from the fitters' attitude they were always pleased to see the back of them.

Bolton fitters told me the main steam pipe joints at the bottom of the smokebox often blew out on these locomotives, and the access to them was very restricted. They also alleged this was due to the relative movement between the cylinder castings, claiming that both the 4–6–0 and 4–6–4 types had failed with depressing regularity all over the Lancashire & Yorkshire railway system in an earlier decade, due to steam blows from these joints. Seven of both types were allocated to Newton Heath depot, and someone there found a cure for this malady: a dam of fireclay was built around the joints at the bottom of the smokebox and this reservoir was filled with an alloy of molten lead and white metal. . . .

* * *

Chief Mechanical engineers of the L.& Y. had always favoured marine–type big ends and Joy valve gear for their inside cylinder locomotives. When I first encountered this longitudinal bolt method of securing big end brasses, I thought it a great idea – there was no heavy "strap" to lift on and off the crankpin, merely two large castellated nuts to unscrew from the 2½″ diameter bolts, after which the comparatively light arrangement of bolts and retaining plate could be handled with ease.

But a few years experience with marine big ends at Bolton taught me the pitfall awaiting anyone who failed to ensure these nuts and bolts were properly secured during re–assembly. To fail to do so meant that, within a few trips, the bolt threads would become so distorted from the pounding they received that to remove the nuts would need several hours of swinging a sledge hammer against a huge, recessed ring spanner.

From time to time, certain sheds earned for themselves the reputation of being slipshod in the way they maintained steam engines, and during my time at Bolton an important ex–L.& Y. shed in a Lancashire coastal town had a very bad name. It was a driver's repair card reporting "loose big end bolts" on an 0–6–0 3F belonging to this depot which taught me the first lesson about loose bolts in marine big ends. . . .

The ex–L.&Y. 2–4–2 tank locomotives had a design of coupled wheel springing so arranged that, when it became necessary to renew a broken spring, a great cursing could sometimes be heard and many new, exciting four–letter words were invented by fitters and their mates. . . .

There were two small seven–plate laminated springs under each coupled wheel. These were bolted together through holes in the ends of the top plates to form an elliptical shape, which then fitted into a heavy rectangular frame beneath each axlebox, and load adjustment was by means of an 1¾″ diameter setbolt screwed up through a threaded hole in the bottom of the frame.

To renew a spring: first lift the locomotive on jacks, slacken the setbolt and now the ellipse of springs can be lifted out of the frame and renewed; no pins to knock out – just this setbolt to slacken, and to screw back to the same adjustment under the new springs. . . .
But, as with threads on big end bolts, the threads of these axle weight adustment setbolts withstood quite a pounding, became distorted and difficult to turn.

Whilst working a 10/0pm Saturday night shift, during a daily examination of a 2–4–2 tank we found a broken coupled wheel spring, but after jacking the engine up to renew it, we were unable to budge the setbolt, which left me with no alternative but to ask the foreman to provide a fresh engine.

Leading fitter Taylor was a kind, thoughtful man and he kept this locomotive in for me to work on when I arrived at 7.0am on Monday – a pleasant gesture for which I thanked him. . . .

The wheel drop was in use, which deprived us of the alternative method of removing the wheelset, so we had to set about drilling the setbolt out of the frame *in situ,* with a manually–operated rachet drill. Using the breakdown van's oxy–acetylene torch, we burned the setbolt off flush with the bottom of the frame. Then the drill was set up in the pit on a support of timber packings. and the work of drilling began – we had about 2½″ of 1¾″ diameter setbolt to get through. . . . We started with a ½″ diameter drill, followed that with one of 1″ dia. and finished with an 1⅜″. After this drill finished its work,it was necessary to chip the remaining "shell" out with a round–nose chisel, taking care not to damage the threads.

A few of Aspinall's 0–6–0 saddle tanks were allocated to Bolton and these were the only "simple" vacuum–braked locomotives I ever encountered. These must also have been the only engines built solely for shunting with a screw reversing gear – but what a screw! It had a four–start thread which needed only two revolutions of the hand–wheel to reverse the valve gear.

The piston rod packings on these locos were of primitive design, consisting only of two semi–circular white metal rings, approximately 3″ long, coned at each end and bored internally to suit the rod diameter, and externally to fit in the stuffing box. At the cylinder end of the latter the packing seated on a coned brass ring. This assemblage was held in position by a brass gland, which was secured by nuts and locknuts on two long threaded studs. When steam blows occurred with this arrangement, fitters slacked the locking nuts and screwed the gland up a little tighter. Split white metal packing rings of about ½″ thickness were provided for insertion into the stuffing box – and very difficult to withdraw. The time–honoured method was an extremely noisy one which called for the boiler to be at full pressure, the crankpin on bottom dead centre with the brakes hard on, scotches under the wheels, and the regulator opened wide with the motion in reverse gear – and all this to happen outside the clerical office door at the top of No.1 pit in Bolton shed!

The structure of Bolton shed had always appeared quite sound to me, and I'm quite certain the roof did not leak rain as much as that at Swansea Victoria, so it was something of a surprise when one day a gang of men began to knock the place down. The wooden roof was supported on cast iron pillars and demolition began in easy stages. The foreman in charge of the demolition was a painstaking man who knew exactly which part of the roof would fall after his men had sawn through certain roof timbers. He would then arrange for the use of a loco, slip one end of a hefty chain around a selected cast iron pillar and the other over the engine draw–bar hook. After making certain everyone was clear, he'd wave to the driver, who would move his engine for a good old tug at the pillar, which always snapped off like a carrot, bringing down the prescribed section of shed roof.

One day another, more ambitious, foreman arrived to take command. By this time the roof over roads numbered 9,10,11 and 12 had been demolished and loaded into wagons. Under the previous regime, men had been ordered out of the shed during demolition, but locomotives which were left in position on adjoining roads had been quite safe. A brick wall separated roads 1 to 4 from those numbered 5 to 12 and the new foreman was about to demolish the roof above No.8 road; a host of locomotives, steamed up ready to work evening rush hour services, stood marshalled in their correct order of departure on roads 5 and 6.

Everyone was ordered out of the shed, and the chain was passed round a cast–iron pillar and secured over the tender drawbar hook of a Fowler 0–8–0 7F. The driver moved off slowly to take up the slack, but the 7F seemed to baulk at snapping this pillar off, when less powerful locos had succeeded first go. The loco backed off a foot or two before taking the strain again, and to those of us who were watching, the entire shed roof appeared to move. . . .

Then the driver must have opened the regulator wider and the driving wheels slipped; perhaps he then opened the steam sand valve, for there came that familiar metallic grinding sound as the wheels regained traction.

The whole shed quivered like a person teetering on the edge of a precipice for a second; then the entire roof, which still remained over roads 5 to 8, collapsed with a mighty roar and a vast cloud of dust rose up. When it settled, it was obvious the locos on 5 and 6 were so deeply buried beneath the debris it would be impossible to extricate them in time to work their trains.

This disaster was caused by the new foreman's decision not to waste time sawing through the 12″ square timber beams, which were supported by the cast–iron pillars. As a result, when the powerful 0–8–0 finally succeeded in disturbing one pillar, the complete roof toppled as a single unit.

The shed foreman, Sam Knowles, dashed out of his office and gazed white–faced at the scene. When I met him years later and we spoke of this incident, he told me that when he explained to Control why he wanted replacement locos for the evening trains, at first they had simply refused to believe him. . . .

* * *

The rebuilding of the shed roof proceeded apace and in a remarkably short period of three or four months things had returned almost to normal. It had followed a style which utilised standard pre–cast concrete units common to a host of re–constructed L.M.S. sheds after the war. The offices, stores, messrooms and fitting shop which adjoined the shed were not rebuilt. Presumably, the timbers of these roofs had remained sound since they were not impregnated by the smoke and steam from locomotives.

During 1946 the D.L.S. at Newton Heath inquired if I was prepared to move for promotion, and in the belief he was referring to a salaried position, I replied in the affirmative.

Two months later I received a letter advising me to report to the D.L.S. at Rugby, on the following Monday, to receive instructions in the duties of my new post as fitter in charge at Leighton Buzzard. The rate of pay would be 109s/6d. per week (eight shillings a week more than a fitter!), plus an additional 25/– a week lodging allowance. . . .

In the knowledge that refusal meant relegation from the First Division of the promotion league table, on the Monday before Easter I set off for Rugby and found my way to the District Loco Superintendent's office in the shed. There I learned that Mr. Mercer had been called away on urgent business and had left word for me to continue on to Bletchley shed, where all would be revealed.

When I arrived at the latter I explained to the shed foreman that the D.L.S. had been called away on business of vital importance. He gazed at me with a rather sceptical expression. "I know!" he exclaimed, with heavy sarcasm. "I've just seen him in his overalls, firing a "Prince of Wales" on the 12/40 Rugby – Euston !"

"That's the train I've travelled on!" I said.

"You should have ridden on the engine – he would have explained your duties, between shovelling coal into the firebox!" he replied.

Apparently, the D.L.S. had a penchant for shovelling coal into locomotive fireboxes. . . .

Bletchley was only six miles north of Leighton Buzzzard and was, for several years following the war, a very important railway centre. The crosscountry lines between Cambridge and Oxford were utilised intensively for freight traffic, which had to be filtered across the busiest main line in the world at Bletchley station, and severe delays were inevitable. Even in 1946, one heard railwaymen of all grades discoursing on the need for a "fly–over" connection between the Oxford and Cambridge lines, and eventually this was built, but by the time it was opened the need for it was already diminishing.

This heavy cross–country traffic brought a demand for staff of all grades, but Bletchley was in a rural area and this could only be met by the process of loaning men from other depots for higher grade duties. For example: several passed cleaners were on loan from Swansea, where they rarely had a firing turn; at Bletchley they were guaranteed regular firing work, and this was the carrot used to induce staff of all grades to work temporarily at Bletchley.

Accommodating scores of itinerant workers in a small place like Bletchley was a problem the L.M.S. solved by using a rake of second class compartment corridor stock as sleeping accommodation for these men, with a kitchen car and dining car to provide a meal service.

The shed foreman went into some detail to describe my duties at Leighton Buzzard; apparently, Bletchley provided four Super Ds and one 5′6″ tank to work at Leighton, and there were ten sets of enginemen at the shed to work the morning and afternoon services. There should also have been three passed cleaners and three labourers, but staff recruitment in the area was very difficult and there were no cleaners, and only two labourers at the moment.

I was surprised to discover that Aylesbury shed was also my responsibility. Bletchley provided a 5′6″ tank to work there, and there were two sets of enginemen, plus a passed cleaner on night duty to look after the engine. As the 5′6″ worked passenger trains I would have to travel to Aylesbury every day to examine this engine.

The foreman reserved his *pièce de résistance* until last. Carefully observing my reaction, he announced that since all the engines would be in the shed overnight, the D.L.S. had decreed I must work a regular night shift. . . .

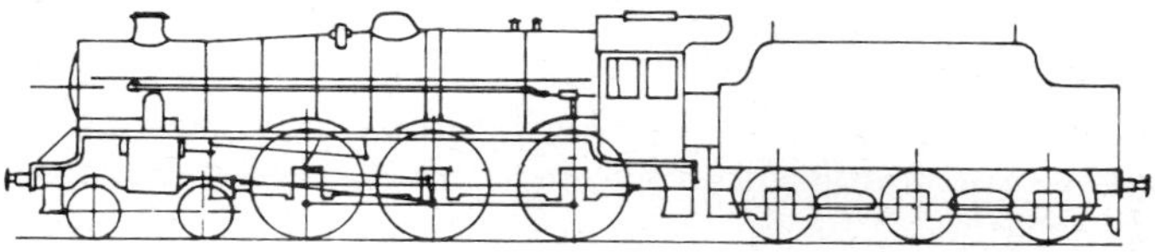

CHAPTER VIII
Post War Years

It took me six weeks to find digs in Leighton Buzzard, and for that period I slept in the coaches stabled in the Bletchley carriage sidings, along with scores of other railwaymen; it was not a happy experience.

By the time I moved to my new digs I had found a good reason to request a change in my turn of duty to one of daywork: it was impossible to get to Aylesbury, examine the 5′6″ and get back without incurring overtime each day. When the D.L.S. pointed out these duties could be covered by a shift which began at 2.0a.m. and ended at 11.00a.m, I replied this was an unacceptable alternative – I awaited his reaction with bated breath!

He agreed to a daywork shift, providing I could show that locomotive repairs and adjustments would not suffer in consequence. The 5′6″ and two Super D turns came on shed to change crews each day and alternating the four Super Ds on these turns I could inspect these engines every other day, and carry out any repairs that might be necessary; that suggestion satisfied the D.L.S.'s requirements.

Most of the freight traffic at Leighton Buzzard consisted of chalk, quarried from the Dunstable Downs at a place called Stanbridgeford, the intermediate station between Leighton and Dunstable, Each day five trains of wagons loaded with chalk at this quarry arrived in Leighton yard, to be marshalled into trains destined for Rugby Portland Cement factories. These had increased to seven trains each day by the time I left a year later.

The distance between the quarry at Stanbridgeford and Leighton was about six miles. The line was fairly level for the last mile or so and this allowed the Super Ds to get these trains rattling along by the time they reached Wing Level Crossing box. Immediately after the level crossing, the tracks swung sharply right and climbed very steeply for the next few hundred yards, as they rose to the level of the main line in Leighton. As soon as the crossing box came abeam, drivers were in the habit of winding the valve gear into full travel and opening the the regulator wide for a real thrash up the gradient into the marshalling yard: that was the only way to ensure these heavy trains surmounted this short but steep bank. Wing Crossing Box up distant signal was of the fixed variety; in other words, it was fixed permanently in the caution position, thus constantly warning drivers that the next signal in advance might be at danger. With the engine in full throat up this sharp incline, drivers would move over to the fireman's side in order to catch an early glimpse of the home signal, which protected the goods line and local platform.

I could see the signal from the window of my office, and hear the often uneven eruptions from the chimneys of the unleashed Super Ds as they charged up the gradient; if the signal stood at danger, I always went outside for a good view of what I knew would happen next. . . .

As soon as the driver spotted the danger signal, over would go the vacuum brake handle for a full application – there was no time or room for a gentle application to gather the wagons together first – all the anchors had to be dropped at once! The reaction of the loose–coupled wagons to this rough treatment would often cause one or two of the three–link couplings to snap apart, but guards were just as aware of this possibility as the drivers, and would be ready to prevent any run–back by applying the hand brake of the goods brake van. The up line at this point was sprinkled about by dozens of snapped links from the loose couplings of chalk wagons.

Leighton enginemen on early turn brought these chalk trains into the sidings, where they were marshalled into trains for afternoon departure, worked by our late shift enginemen. Leighton men worked a chalk train via Blisworth to Northampton, but we considered the one which ran chalk to Southam and Long Itchington our most important train. This travelled over the main line to Weedon, where it took the route which branched to the west through Daventry, Braunston, Flecknoe, Napton and Stockton to the cement works at Southam and Long Itchington. This line then ran via Leamington Spa and Warwick to Kenilworth, from where one branch ran to Coventry and another joined the Coventry – Birmingham main line at Berkswell.

The heaviest chalk train of all was hauled from Leighton Buzzard by an engine which ran light from Bletchley, in charge of Bletchley enginemen. This departed after midnight and was routed over a chord line connection, about a mile south of Bletchley, onto the Oxford branch, where it was handed to the G.W.R. Access to the chord line was off the down fast line only, and so this train was turned out through the slow to fast junction controlled by Leighton No.2 signal box.

This was said to be the heaviest freight then running over the Western Division of the L.M.S. south of Crewe. It consisted of a brake van and about seventy wagons, each loaded with an unspecified tonnage of chalk (usually much in excess of the wagons registered capacity) and all the wagon axles were fitted with bearings lubricated by grease.

As this train started from Leighton Buzzard, it turned out of a siding on to the up slow, then negotiated an up slow to down crossing, ran through the station and traversed the down slow to down fast connection. The length of these trains was such that the rear end would still be negotiating the curves of the up slow to down slow connection. This caused an additional friction between wheel flanges and rail which imposed an unusually heavy load on the loco, even when the grease in the wagon axleboxes was warmed by a balmy summer's night. When winter frosts hardened the grease, the rolling resistance of these wagons became enormous, and the Super D often ground to a halt half way across the slow to fast line connection. Bletchley Control would then have to issue a "Wrong Line Order," permitting a driver to take his engine up the down fast line from Bletchley to Leighton Buzzard to assist the stalled train.

Our 5′6″ tank maintained an hourly passenger service between Leighton Buzzard and Dunstable, with morning and evening trains extended to the L.N.E.R. station in Luton. The platform shared the same roof as the L.M.S. station, but there appeared to be no physical connection between the lines.

Whenever the 5′6″ tanks were in short supply, Bletchley often provided an L.N.W. 0–6–2T as a replacement. The first time it happened, the Bletchley foreman rang me to say he was sending a "Watford" tank to replace our 5′6″, which was due for "X" scheme. Not wishing to display my ignorance, I told him I would make the necessary arrangement, and waited to see what a "Watford" tank looked like. . . .

It was during the exceptionally cold spell in the winter of 1946–47 when the "Watford" tank arrived. It was the first of its type I had seen; it looked exactly like a Cauliflower, but was an 0–6–2T with side tanks and a radial truck.

This loco worked an afternoon train to Dunstable, ran round the coaches and worked bunker–first back to Leighton. On arrival in the station the driver rang me to announce the locomotive steam brake had failed. I gathered some tools and walked up to see him; he explained he'd discovered this defect after uncoupling from the coaches, preparatory to running round in the station. The copper steam pipe to the brake cylinder ran beneath the footplate, in a position which exposed it to a blast of cold air when running bunker–first, and it had frozen on the journey from Dunstable.

We thawed it out, but I decided to take the loco on shed to lag the pipe, even though this meant delaying the train. Despite assistance from the enginemen the train left some twenty minutes late, resulting in the need to initiate a "Locomotive Mechanical Casualty Report". This was a mandatory requirement in cases where a loco lost five or more minutes working a passenger train, or ten or more with a goods train, due to a mechanical defect.

Literally thousands of these documents, each bearing its own tale of woe, must have passed through the hands of dozens of engineers in positions of authority, but in the vast majority of instances no action was ever taken to improve the design of components.

* * *

I caught the 10.25 local from Leighton Buzzard to Cheddington each day, and walked across the overbridge spanning the slow and fast lines to the Aylesbury platform, where the 5′6″ 2–4–2T would be waiting with its solitary coach, ready to leave for Aylesbury. If any wagons or vans required conveyance to Aylesbury. these would be attached with a brake van at the rear of the train.

The distance between Cheddington and Aylesbury was approximately ten miles, all single track with one intermediate stop, Marston Gate halt. On arrival at Aylesbury the coach would be put aside, and any necessary shunting of wagons performed for the traffic department, before the engine was taken to the shed for my inspection.

Occasionally, the brake would require adjustment, a small gland repacking or a sand valve opening, but I never found any defect of a serious nature. The two sets of enginemen worked alternate morning and afternoon turns and they looked after this engine most carefully – very much as drivers did years ago, when each man kept his own engine, and once a fortnight a "shed day" was allotted to the engine and driver, to allow him to pack footplate glands as well as oversee any other repairs which fitters were carrying out.

During my twelve months at Leighton Buzzard there were two major locomotive failures. The first of these happened as a Super D ran into Leighton Buzzard from Northampton with a train of empties for the chalk quarries. As the loco propelled the wagons into the yard clear of the main line, there was a loud bang from the front end and a roar of steam up the chimney; it was brought on to the shed for my inspection. I discovered the right hand piston was defective, and set about removing the front cylinder cover; surprisingly, many of the nuts were only finger tight. Because the cover was too heavy for one man to handle, and at this period I had no assistance available, I had to "bar" it off the studs and allow it to fall onto wooden packing on the pit. The

Super D No. 8899 photographed on Salop (L.M.S.) shed in June 1947. This was one of the class fitted with a 'back-cab' tender but is still retaining its original L.N.W.R. dry sand valves; a likely explanation is that the tender has been changed.
(Photo: H.C. Casserley)

Royal Train loco No. 48309 at Llandovery on 23 October 1952. Note the polished buffers, drawbar, cylinder and steam chest covers on this 8F.

One of the 2-8-0 8Fs on shed at Paxton Street, Swansea.

A typical array of shunting engines on shed at Newton Heath in April 1951. Fowler 3FT No. 47577 (without vacuum brake) obscures an Aspinall 2F 0-6-0ST (rebuilt from a Barton Wright 0-6-0), whilst two similar saddle tanks stand on the adjoining road.

large nut which secured the head onto the piston rod had become detached and trapped at the bottom of the cylinder cover studs round the bottom of the cylinder cover. The 7/8″ dia. cylinder cover studs round the bottom of the cylinder had been stretched like elastic by the impact of the piston head against the nut and cover, but miraculously none had been broken – and the cylinder cover was quite intact. I had a struggle to remove the piston head, which was wedged at an angle in the front of the cylinder, but eventually it, too, fell into the pit, apparently little worse for the experience apart from rings broken by the fall.

After having this loco dragged up the shed yard to ensure the headless piston rod would move freely in the gland packing, arrangements were made to have it towed to Bletchley. A few days later a down goods halted on the slow line, its loco came to shed to collect the crippled Super D and I travelled with it to Bletchley. The leading fitter told me the Shopping Bureau at Derby had already accepted this engine for intermediate repairs and, after wiring it "out of service", he expected it to be called into shops within a few days.

Each class of locomotive was given a time period between overhaul in main works. A few weeks before the expiration of the time period the locomotive was specially inspected and the results of this examination recorded on a "Shopping Proposal Form," which also called for a history of the locomotive and boiler, together with a mileage run since last Intermediate or General repair.

The Proposal Form was sent to the Shopping Bureau at Derby, and the decision to accept the loco into works, or extend the period for a few months, would be based on a variety of factors; mileage run since last shops or condition of locomotive and boiler as stated on proposal form. Quite often the requirements of Boiler Inspection would be the over–riding factor in this decision.

If the shopping period was to be extended the proposal form would be returned with a re–proposal date stamped thereon. Acceptance for Works overhaul was by means of an advisory notice stating that if any heavy repair or mileage examination became necessary the Shopping Bureau must be advised at once.

After a locomotive was accepted for works it was depot practice to allow it another month or two in traffic before sending a plaintive telegram to the Shopping Bureau: "Locomotive withdrawn from traffic due to excessive wear in axleboxes" was a theme guaranteed to tug at the heartstrings of the Shopping Bureau, and within a few days shopping instructions would arrive.

★ ★ ★

I was allowed free travel facilities to Little Hulton each week–end, and, although the opportunity was afforded every Sunday to work at Bletchley shed as a fitter, I preferred to get home whenever possible. There was always some doubt about this free travel entitlement, and enquiries in several quarters rather tended to indicate the dispensation of free passes to a non–salaried fitter–in–charge was at the discretion of the chief clerk; ergo – be nice to that gentleman! A driver at Leighton Buzzard was able to conjure up an occasional supply of "off–the–ration" eggs and butter, half of which went to aid the free pass position. But in case the supply dried up, I went to great pains to avoid having these free passes clipped by ticket inspectors. Whilst the method used now escapes me, the memory of the comforting feel of a half–dozen small, unsullied, oblongs of cardboard always in the pocket lingers on.

Each Saturday I caught an 11.30 local from Leighton to Bletchley, and a Euston to Blackpool express from there to Crewe. There was a choice of routes from Crewe: a local into Manchester London Rd. and by tram car to Exchange, for a local train to Little Hulton station. Alternatively, continue on the Blackpool express to Wigan L.N.W. where a short walk across the town brought one to Wigan Wallgate station, to await a train to Walkden H.L.station.

Staff began to drift away from railway employment, particularly in the Leighton area, and after a few months only one aged labourer remained at Leighton shed and he had to work a regular night turn as "steamraiser". I had no staff to keep the place clean, or to perform any chores, but more important, no–one to coal engines when they arrived on shed with part–empty tenders at night. It was this job of shovelling about 20 tons of coal from wagons into tenders every night that put every labouring recruit off the job after only a few days.

Eventually, it became accepted practice at Leighton Buzzard for enginemen to re-coal their own locomotives – after they had dropped the fire and shovelled the ash out of the smokeboxes. Only on one occasion did depot bureaucracy question the amount of overtime the enginemen booked to this duty, and the clerk responsible was rapidly silenced, by a management fearful that any hint of pecuniary restraint might stop the coaling altogether.

During my few weeks of night work there was a short period each night one came to enjoy, between six and seven o'clock every morning, after locos had gone off shed and everywhere was comparatively peaceful.

When first I heard the odd pulsating sound I was unable to account for it, except by attributing it to some new type of fast–revving i/c engine running at an unvarying speed. It was only audible on those calm, still spring mornings when mists hang gossamer–like over the meadows. The realisation dawned that this strange noise was caused by the exhaust beats of locomotives working the overnight sleeping car trains from the north towards Euston. This strange effect was more a throbbing of air than a sound, caused probably by the masking action of Linslade Hill just north of the station, through which the tunnels were drilled.

There were three tunnels at Linslade, all only a few hundred yards long. The up slow was a single line bore, the middle bore carried the down slow and up fast line, and the down fast line also had a single bore tunnel.

The relatively restricted aperture of the latter tunnel frequently caused problems for engines entering it at high speed. It was claimed that loose footplate floor boarding frequently became displaced, thus hazarding any firemen who might be shovelling coal at that moment. Loose cab window glass was an obvious danger and I can attest that the unsecured lids of Silvertown mechanical lubricators stood no chance of surviving passage through this tunnel. Every few weeks the P.W. ganger responsible for the length sent me a sack of material recovered from the track inside the down fast line tunnel; broken lids of mechanical lubricators went onto our scrap iron heap, but we had an almost constant supply of rubber lids off sand boxes recovered from this source, which we returned to Camden loco shed.

★ ★ ★

I visited Bletchley shed one morning each week to replenish my unofficial stock of consumable parts, such as split cotters, split pins, nuts and bolts. The shortest, although unofficial, route from station to shed was via the timbered pathway which crossed the tracks beyond the platform ramps at the north end. One morning, as I waited on the crossing, a stopping train headed by a "Lizzie" ran into the station on the up fast line, and as it ran past me I was certain I had caught a glimpse of a defective bissel truck spring. I hurried down the long train, arriving at the locomotive just as the driver received the "right away" from the guard. The rear pillar bolt of the bissel truck spring was missing, and with its load released, that end of the spring was cocked up at an awkward angle; there was no alternative course other than to fail this locomotive and ask Control to provide a fresh engine.

The driver said he had not felt anything unusual about the riding characteristics of the Pacific, and when Control could find no better replacement than an L.N.W. 4–6–0 "Prince of Wales," he voiced the opinion it would be better if outsiders kept their noses out of other people's business ! Nor was he alone in this – the station foreman and shunters positively glowered as they attached the 4–6–0 to the train. The hostility of the delayed passengers was also almost tangible and I crept into Bletchley shed, thinking that at least here I would find some reward for my alertness – but nothing of the sort! Instead, the leading fitter inquired if I thought he'd nothing better to do than change springs on Camden engines. . . .

Another serious failure happened about seven o'clock one evening, only a few weeks before I left Leighton Buzzard. It was my habit to spend a couple of hours each evening by either riding on the footplate of the 7/5pm to Luton and back, or in Leighton Buzzard No.1 signalbox. I was making my way towards that box when I observed a "Baby Scot" and its train halted on the down fast line a few hundred yards south of No.1 box. As I walked past, the signalman called down to advise me that Bletchley breakdown train was on its way to the scene.

The locomotive was an unnamed parallel–boiler Patriot, No.5508, at that time allocated to Preston Maudland shed, which had "dropped" its left hand bottom slidebar and wreaked havoc to that side of the motion. The piston rod was badly distorted, a section of the back cylinder cover had broken away and the connecting rod would have to be dismantled before the loco could be moved. I walked across the main line to the shed, donned my overalls and collected a few tools; as I went back towards the cripple I was relieved to see the Bletchley breakdown train emerging from the up slow tunnel at Linslade. Without any help from me, the breakdown gang removed the connecting rod, secured the L.H.valve in mid–position and 5508 was uncoupled from the train of parcel vans and eased across the main line under its own steam into the goods yard. Delays to main line services were considerable, for the parcels train had come to rest over the points of the down fast to down slow line connection, and a following passenger train was halted at Sears Crossing box for quite some time before the down fast line was re–opened.

5508 went to Bletchley with the breakdown train and when I saw this loco in the shed two days later, fitters were at work dismantling all the motion. The L.H. cylinder casting was found to be fractured and the locomotive had been "wired out of service" and special shopping proposal forms were already in the post to Derby Shopping Bureau. Headquarters' Inspectors had established the cause of this failure as loose nuts on the front slide bar studs, which eventually allowed the L.H. bottom slide bar to become displaced.

★ ★ ★

Signalmen were paid according to the classification of the signalbox in which they were employed. "Special" class boxes were the busiest, followed by class 1,2,3 and 4 boxes. Leighton Buzzard No.1 and 2 were both in the class 1 category, and from what one saw of the activities of these men, the rating was fully justified. This was so on morning turn, when they hardly had time to eat their sandwiches, and would have to ask for relief before they could visit the toilet.

Two of the signalmen in No.1 box were pleasant middle–aged men, but the third was a very large gentleman approaching retirement age, a xenophobe renowned for the irascibility of his temperament, which he sometimes vented with a ponderous clenched fist – a blow most of his workmates had learned to dodge. But the Irish goods guard from Willesden, who had a pronounced brogue and a tendency to fall asleep on duty, failed to take evasive action and felt it's full force one night at Leighton Buzzard. . . .

During the hours of darkness goods brake vans displayed three "tail lamps", one each side of the vehicle and the third on the buffer plank, in a "vee" configuration. When travelling on the up slow line, the tail lamp next to the up fast line had to display a white aspect and if the goods was crossed to the fast line, the guard must alter the white aspect to the opposite side of the brake van. Of course, the same regulation applied to trains in the down direction, its purpose being to enable drivers of express trains to readily identify which line the goods train they were about to overtake was occupying.

A goods train which left Willesden about midnight for Swanbourne sidings, on the Bletchley – Oxford line, was turned out on to the fast line at Tring. The Cheddington signalman observed the position of the white tail lamp had not been altered for fast line travel and rang Leighton No.1 box. The Leighton signalman brought the engine of the goods train to a halt outside his box and instructed the driver to draw forward and stop with the brake van opposite his box – an almost impossible task for the driver of a long train to achieve with any degree of accuracy. In fact, when the train came to a halt the brake van was some distance beyond No.1 box and despite a voice of stentorian power, the signalman could get no response from the goods guard, and was forced to leave his box and walk to the brake van in blizzard conditions.

Some time later, the signalman displayed a green hand lamp to the driver and the train left with tail lamps now in the correct position.

The run from Leighton to Swanbourne Sidings was no more than ten miles and probably of less than thirty minutes duration. The Willesden guard and enginemen were rostered to be relieved on arrival by a crew who worked the train forward, but when the relief guard entered the brake van he discovered his collegue in a dazed and badly bruised condition, and elucidated that these injuries had been inflicted by a maniacal signalman at Leighton Buzzard. The local foreman decided to send the injured man to hospital.

The District Operating Superintendent held an inquiry into the incident, and the Leighton stationmaster showed me a transcript of these proceedings: the signalman said the guard had been asleep when he entered the brakevan and he'd given him a good old "scuff" across the ears to wake him up. But then the man swore at him in an Irish brogue and being incensed by the idea of having to leave the cosy warmth of his cabin to wake up an Irishman, he admitted to losing his temper and letting fly. He was suspended from duty for three days. . . .

During March of 1947 I received a letter asking if I was prepared to accept the post of Mechanical Foreman at Swansea, of all places: the same day I replied signifying assent! Next, I was sent to Drummond Street, Euston, for a medical examination and a few days later my replacement arrived – a fitter, aged about fifty, from Springs Branch shed at Wigan. I spent two days showing him the routine, and he was obviously delighted with the place, claiming nothing would ever induce him to leave Leighton Buzzard. I heard several years later that this fitter had entered into the spirit of the community to a far greater degree than myself and my informant added that in fact he eventually become mayor of the town.

* * *

When I arrived at Swansea I found I was the first salaried foreman to have been appointed there. All the previous appointees had been wages staff leading fitters and I never discovered the reason for this policy change. Conceivably, it could have been because of the improved supervisory status of the person in charge, who was now an assistant District Locomotive Superintendent, responsible to the Superintendent at Shrewsbury for Builth Road, Llandovery, Carmarthen, Upper Bank and Gurnos. The wheel had turned almost a full cycle in the fourteen years since the appointment of Tommy Follows!

Only one fitter remained of those who had been at Victoria shed when I left in 1941 – Phil Plant. All the rest had moved away for promotion, but he had more sense than most of us and had refused to leave his small cottage in Oystermouth and the fishing boat he owned, moored only a few hundred yards from his front door. . . .

The locomotive allocation at Swansea Victoria in 1947 was as follows:

2-4-2T	1P	L.N.W.R.	1890	5′8½″	Webb	4
0-6-2T	2F	L.N.W.R.	1882	4′5½″	Webb	5
0-6-0	2F	L.N.W.R.	1887	5′2½″	Webb	1
0-8-4T	7F	L.N.W.R.	1923	4′5½″	Beames	3
0-0-0	7F	L.N.W.R.	1921	4′5½″	Bowen Cooke	8
0-6-0T	1F	M.R.	1878	4′7″	Johnson	1
2-6-4T	4P	L.M.S.	1927	5′9″	Fowler	7
2-8-0	8F	L.M.S.	1935	4′8½″	Stanier	12
					Total	41

Apart from the very welcome addition of a dozen Stanier 2–8–0 8Fs, the loco stock at Swansea and Upper Bank had not changed a great deal. The ex–M.R. 0–6–0 3Fs Nos.3389 and 3657 had been transferred and the solitary Cauliflower, 58622, worked only for a few weeks after my arrival before it was accepted for Shops and I sent a telegram to the Shopping Bureau, wiring it out of service due to worn condition of axleboxes. In point of fact, the axleboxes on these locos were virtually trouble–free but the Shopping Bureau accepted my *faux pas* without comment. 58622 stood at the bottom of No.6 road for several months before being called into shops, and then I believe it was for cutting–up.

With the allocation of the Stanier 2–8–0s there was no longer any need for a stud of 2–6–0 "Crabs". The 2–8–0s were quite able to keep time with passenger trains over the Central Wales, and the "Crabs" had been re–allocated.

The fitting staff complement had remained numerically static, but there were many unfamiliar faces and several fitters came from backgrounds without railway tradition.

The ancient belt–driven machinery had been replaced by a new combination plain lathe, shaper and heavy duty drill. There was a 6″ screw cutting lathe, a high speed drilling machine, a tool grinder, plus a new gas–fired metalling hearth.

After I had been at Swansea a few months Reg Smith paid me an official visit. He had now risen to be Divisional Mechanical Inspector at Crewe and his prime responsibility was to ensure that all loco sheds in the Western Division of the L.M.S. were carrying out "Standard Practices" in the manner prescribed. Each locomotive was provided with two Standard Examination Cards which lasted for a twelve month period. On these, brief details were printed of each item requiring periodic or mileage examination on every type of locomotive on the L.M.S. One card provided space to record details of the condition of individual wheels and tyres: e.g.: H⅛″ in the appropriate space, indicated the tread on the tyre of the wheel in that position had worn ⅛″ hollow. A letter T entered in the space signified the tyre flange was wearing thin. L meant the tyre was loose on the wheel centre.

Fitters signed and dated in the appropriate column against the item they had examined during period or mileage examination, and space was provided on the reverse side of the "Wheel & Tyre" card to record daily or weekly examination of the loco, and the renewal or examination of firebox fusible lead plugs.

On these two 18″ squares of cardboard was the maintenance history of the locomotive. The 3 to 5 week and 7 to 9 week periodic examination dates were there for all to see, as was the mileage at which each mileage examination had been carried out, and all this information was ambrosia to the Divisional Inspectors.

Decent family men like Reg Smith were transformed into Jekyll and Hyde characters as soon as they were appointed to these positions. The mere sight of a pile of Examination Cards turned them into sadists of the worst kind, and these cards contained all the information they needed to practice their Black Art of "Standard Practice Investigations".

The result of Reg Smith's investigation at Swansea cast a black shadow over the depot's performance, particularly with regard to mileage examinations, many of which had been allowed to over–run by as much as a thousand miles since I had taken over at Swansea.

Mileage examinations were carried out at increments of between five and six thousand miles and it was the responsibility of the depot mileage clerk to advise me when a locomotive had run four thousand miles since its previous examination. From then it was my responsibility to have the work carried out within the prescribed mileage limits, and obviously I had been under–estimating the mileage run by the different classes of locomotive we had. I explained my difficulty to the 17–year old typist–cum–mileage clerk, who inquired if I would care to continue the close relationship which had existed between herself and my predecessor. This prospect delighted me, but I felt in her own interests I should mention that I was a married man. . . . It hadn't been *that* sort of relationship, she replied primly. Apparently, at the behest of the former leading fitter, when an examination over–ran, she had deducted sufficient mileage to bring the recorded figure within the limits, and added the over–run miles to the next examination. But there were pitfalls in this arrangement which could be uncovered by anyone who wished to delve deeply into records, and what I needed was a reasonably accurate figure of average daily mileage run by each type of locomotive at Swansea. The young lady provided me with this data, after which there were very few subsequent instances of over–run mileage examinations at Swansea.

A vacancy for a fitter occurred a few months after I arrived at Swansea and we were fortunate to engage an excellent man named Munroe, who had served an apprenticeship at the L.M.S. St.Rollox Works in Glasgow, afterwards spending several years at sea before settling down in Pontardawe.

The frequency of hot axles occurring on the Swansea stud of Gadgets had not lessened during my absence – if anything these axleboxes were running hot more often. The Assistant D.L.S. would not allow me to send a wheelset to main works for journal turning, on the grounds that he could not spare the loco out of service for that length of time. When I pointed out it was impossible to fit a new bearing on such a badly scored journal, he approached the turner and asked him to reproduce the same score marks on the bearing as he bored it in the lathe. . . . The turner's reply was unprintable!

With the help of fitter Munroe, a new way was found to lubricate the leading wheel axleboxes of our Gadgets, in such a manner that sand ingress into the oil wells forged in the axlebox top no longer impeded oil supply to the bearing. A brass oil box of the kind used to lubricate the trailing axleboxes was bolted to each leading wheel splasher and from it a copper pipe ran inside, bracketed on to the main frame. From the bracket a flexible pipe carried oil to a connection in the axlebox. Both axleboxes and the brass bearing steps had to be drilled for the new oil–way and that meant removing each leading wheelset and dismantling the axleboxes for this purpose. It took Bill Munroe and his mate two days to fit this new lubrication system to the leading wheelset of a Gadget, and whilst it did not entirely eradicate overheating, there was a significant reduction in the number of hot leading axleboxes.

We looked at a similar modification for the Gadget driving wheelsets but there was insufficient clearance to fit an oilpipe to these axleboxes, because of the crank axle sweeps.

It took some time to spread word of these new oilboxes among the drivers and we were prevented from publishing an official notice on their "Special Notices" board for political reasons: it was strictly illegal to carry out any modification to a locomotive, or to a component thereof, without first obtaining permission of the C.M.E. and plainly this was a very necessary ordinance for reasons of safety.

We knew the Works people would discover the modification as soon as the first Swansea Gadget went into Shops for programmed overhaul and, although it was a simple task to remove the oil boxes and pipes, the drilled axleboxes would give us away. It was therefore decided to allow the first loco to go to shops with the complete modification, and I sat back and waited for the storm. . . . Munroe and I believed that at least the entire arrangement would be removed and the loco sent back in its original state. But no such thing happened – the Works staff turned that loco out of Crewe Works exactly as we had sent it in, and every other Gadget we sent to shops was treated likewise. The flexible oil pipes were always renewed in Works and on at least one occasion when a new axlebox was fitted, oilways were drilled in it for the Swansea style lubrication.

I had been at Swansea less than a year when the railways were Nationalised, and shortly after this happened it was made known to us that all the L.M.S. lines in South and Central Wales were to be incorporated in the new Western Region. However, agreement had been reached with the Unions that salaried staff would be given two opportunities of transferring back to similar posts on London Midland Region.

I was offered a position as shift mechanical foreman at Bescot and had no hesitation in turning that job down! Next came the offer of a similar post at Crewe North, but on regular daywork with responsibility for valve and piston examinations on Stanier Pacifics.

I was aware that for some time all the 4–6–2 8P locos on the L.M.S. had been sent to Crewe North shed for these examinations, and that specially trained staff plus new equipment had been provided to facilitate the work. This was a further stage in the "concentration depot" idea, and I also knew that agreement had been given for yet another development in the form of a completely new depot at Crewe which would be devoted to carrying out valve and piston examinations not only on Pacifics but also on all the 4–6–0 Royal Scots and subsequently the Patriots, etc. would be included.

Obviously, that would have been a position in which the occupant had a rare chance to build a reputation for himself, but I had made two moves within twelve months and felt a need to settle down for a few years.

The L.M.S. Shrewsbury District locomotive sheds were absorbed by three W.R. Districts at Nationalisation. Swansea, Llandovery, Builth Road, Gurnos and Upper Bank merged into the Neath District; Carmathen shed was closed, with the engines and staff transferred to the G.W.shed. Shrewsbury, Craven Arms, Knighton and Hereford became part of the Wolverhampton District whilst Abergavenny, Tredegar and Blaenavon transferred to the Newport district.

Swansea shed was renamed "Paxton Street" and lost the status it had enjoyed under the L.M.S. regime. The Assistant D.L.S. was moved to a post befitting his rank and we waited to see who would be appointed as his successor.

A few weeks before the Nationalisation vesting date, the L.M.S. authorities began to transfer all the Stanier 8F from Swansea, and they were replaced by W.D. 2–8–0s built during the war for service overseas. The design provided no more than basic standards of comfort for enginemen, which earned the sobriquet "Austerity" for these machines. Whatever may be claimed for their performance, it is cerainly true to say that the footplate provided a greatly reduced level of comfort, and the riding characteristics were inferior to those of the Stanier 2–8–0 engines.

The vacant post at Paxton Street was filled by a Swindon–trained engineer; this was a radical departure from the traditional G.W.R.practise of appointing men from the footplate grades to fill the posts of Locomotive Shed Foreman – posts which were now awarded the more impressive title of "Locomotive Shedmaster".

As a direct result of this preference for depot management by men without formal training in locomotive engineering, the G.W.R. found it necessary to create a hierarchy of Mechanical Inspectors at District level, to whom depot maintenance foreman could refer engineering problems. As all shedmasters on the L.M.S. were appointed from the engineering section, they were the final arbiters in such matters at depot level and no District Mechanical Inspector was necessary.

Of course, protagonists of the G.W. practise will argue that 75 per cent of a Locomotive shedmaster's time was spent dealing with matters affecting the running of trains and footplatemen had first–hand experience of these matters which was denied to men trained as engineers. However, in my admittedly rather limited experience of G.W. loco sheds, I gained a distinct impression that this division of responsibility created a dichotomous situation at some depots.

The shedmaster appointed at Swansea had no depot experience and it was unfortunate he should have to take over at a time when Swansea enginemen were just beginning to react to the effect Nationalisation had upon them. Instead of an improved life style, as they had hoped for, their standards had been worsened by the transfer of the Stanier 8F locomotives, and they were now becoming very vocal about the situation. . . .

After a month or two they began to realise that complaints were useless – action was needed. We began to experience an ever increasing number of "late starts" to trains worked by Austerity 2–8–0s, simply because drivers would refuse to leave the shed unless every part of the loco was in perfect condition. Even more extensive delays were occurring at Llandovery, where Swansea enginemen were relieved by Llandovery crews.

Because of what they claimed to be a dangerous design of fall plate between engine and tender, firemen refused to change single line staffs at the permitted speeds of 10 or 15 m.p.h., and drivers were bringing trains almost to a halt for that purpose, which caused further delay. Eventually, with the backing of the unions, an ultimatum was issued to B.T.C. giving a date beyond which enginemen would refuse to work Austerities over the Central Wales. A meeting was arranged between union and management, during which the latter made a face–saving gesture, offering to appoint an arbiter to assess the suitability of the ex–W.D. engines to work over the line.

When this proposal was put to the Swansea enginemen they rejected it out of hand. However, words were whispered into their ears to indicate the matter was already settled, but management wanted to paper over the cracks. The Southern Region's Chief Motive Power Officer, Mr. Chrimes, carried out a week–long series of riding tests to decide if these locos were fit to work freight trains over the Central Wales. We all knew what the results of these tests would be before he began them. . . . Sure enough, a few weeks later the transfer away of Austerities began, and my inspection of the Stanier 2–8–0 locos which replaced them convinced me that all twelve of these engines had only recently emerged fresh–off shops, and this was confirmed when their records arrived.

Subsequent to the severance of our umbilical with Shrewsbury, we now had to carry out valve and piston examinations on Paxton Street and Upper Bank engines and, since we had found it impossible to engage additional fitters, it became necessary to reduce our work load by any means possible. This objective was achieved by transferring much of the work normally done at depots during these examinations, to Crewe Works Machine Shop.

A weekly stores van from Crewe Works arrived on shed at 4/30pm every Friday. Engines requiring V & P examination were berthed on the "mileage pit" ready for work to start at eight that morning, and by the time the stores van left for Crewe on the 12/35pm passenger on Saturday, it would be loaded with piston valves, crossheads and motion, for overhaul in Crewe Works.

In normal circumstances we could expect the return of this material on the following Friday, which gave us a week to work on the remaining items scheduled for examination during overhaul. But despite the success of this method in reducing our work load, it was still necessary for the fitting staff to work a considerable amount of overtime each week.

Surreptitious checks on our wages bill over several months revealed that after Nationalisation, because of the fact that all the fitting staff now had to work overtime and I did not, my post was the lowest paid of any member of the staff, excluding the two apprentice fitters.

At length, I wrote to the newly appointed (and newly titled) "District Motive Power Superintendent" at Neath, drawing his attention to the discrepancy between my earnings and those of my staff and explaining the reasons why this was so. I received an acknowledgement and learned from a source inside the District H.Q. at Neath that clerical staff there had been instructed to compile an average earnings table for all grades of fitting staff in the Neath District.

Our trainee Shedmaster left mechanical matters to me, and concentrated his mind upon the problems involved in the running of trains, in which, because of his Swindon background, he had had no previous experience. Having been accustomed to the use of micrometers in Swindon Works it must have come as a shock when first he saw calipers being used for this purpose at Paxton Street. I saw him closely watching a fitter machine a pair of big–end brasses in the lathe, then use inside calipers to check the bearing diameter after each tool pass. After a few moments he left the lathe and walked over to speak to me. "What is Bill Munroe doing with those calipers?" he asked. I was taken aback, but I explained how they were used to check the inside diameter of a bearing against the outside diameter of the crankpin, and he went away satisfied.

A few months before he left to take up another post, he accompanied the Paxton Street breakdown train to an accident at Llandovery which might have had tragic results, but in the event proved to be a rather comic affair. After having been coaled, watered and having the fire dropped, a Super D was proceeding from the coal stage to a berth at the bottom of No.3 road in the shed. Boiler steam pressure had fallen to about 801bs, at which pressure the vacuum brake would be powerless, and braking could only be achieved by using the rather inefficient hand brake on the tender. In this instance the 0–8–0 got out of control, ran off the end of the road and across the shed to completely domolish the shedmaster's office, coming to rest with its smokebox buried in the debris of the messroom and lavatory block. Fortunately, no one was injured.

One pair of tender wheels remained on the rails, but I was doubtful what effect pulling the loco back on the rails would have on the rest of the building, for some timbers were draped over the boiler in a manner which suggested the roof might now be relying on it for support.

This incident happened about 5.0a.m, but it was broad daylight before a representative of the District Civil Engineer arrived on the scene to prognosticate upon the likely outcome, and by the time he agreed to pull the loco without first supporting the roof, a crowd had gathered in the field outside the shed.

A Stanier 2–8–0 was used to haul the derailed loco back on the rails, with myself and the D.C.E. representative on the footplate to instruct the driver. As the Super D moved, the entire roof seemed to creak and groan in protest and, remembering the similar incident at the L.& Y. shed in Bolton only a few years earlier, I kept well under the protection of the cab roof, half expecting the same thing to happen on this occasion. But L.N.W. sheds must have been of stronger stuff than those of the L.& Y., for this roof stayed in place. Apart from having to traverse the leading coupled wheels a little before they would run back onto the rails, the sturdy Super D came back on the rails without a murmur and with hardly a scratch to show for her adventure.

Shortly before he left to take up the post of Mechanical Inspector at the W.R.District Head Quarters in Wolverhampton, the shedmaster told me of a serious failure which had occurred to an Abergavenny Super D whilst working a goods train somewhere in the Neath District. This loco had been in the hands of ex–G.W.R. enginemen who had taken over from L.M. men, after which they had only run a few miles before both front cylinder covers burst off and serious damage was inflicted upon the motion and valve gear of the locomotive. On examination no mechanical defect could be found to account for this failure and all the W.R. inspectors were mystified. When I suggested it could have been caused by a driver, inexperienced in handling these locos, opening the regulator too wide with a boiler water level "bobbing" at the top of the gauge glass, he looked at me askance, obviously not in agreement.

I received a letter advising me that the Chief Motive Power Superintendent at Swindon had looked into the points raised in my letter and had decided to lift my post by one grade. This meant an immediate salary increase of approximately £50 p.a. In accordance with the standard arrangements for salary increments, in a further two years one would be entitled to another increment, and four years would pass before one was paid the full salary for the grade.

The next appointee to the post of shedmaster at Paxton Street was a choice which pleased most people at the depot. After serving as apprentice at Paxton Street, during which he reached a high level of scholastic attainment at Swansea Tech., Reg Jenkins had been a fitter for several years before being appointed shedmaster at Upper Bank. His new appointment coincided with the full incorporation of Paxton Street shed into the Neath district and we were henceforth to be included in the "Locomotive Availability League", which was circulated to all depots as part of a monthly newsletter for the District.

The criterion for locomotive availability had long been established as a figure of 85 per cent. A locomotive was deemed not to be available if it was stopped from midnight to midnight. From this it will be seen that a locomotive arriving on shed at 00.05 on, say Monday, and leaving the shed at 23.55 on Tuesday, could be shown in the records as having worked both days, even though during the intervening 47 hours 50 minutes dozens of fitting staff might well have been working on it. . . .

The Neath District Locomotive Availability League was compiled from weekly data submitted by each depot to the B.T.C, and the regulations governing its compilation were those we at Paxton Street had long been accustomed to on the L.M.S., and I suppose this gave us a head start over the G.W.depots.

At that time there were 75 British Railways Motive Power Districts, with Neath District third largest in numbers of engines allocated and ranking with Darlington, Wolverhampton and Newport in having ten codenumbered depots.

Swansea, Paxton Street (87K) was near the top on the very first occasion we were included in the District League, and after a couple of months we were firmly established as league leaders – a position we held for several months. A clerk from the District Office spent some time checking our records but, whilst I was using the rules to full advantage, none were being contravened, and I knew we had nothing to fear from his report. One can imagine the disgruntlement experienced by the G.W.R. District staff at the discovery that the only L.M.S. shed in their district was showing them a clean pair of heels, in a field always considered of prime importance in assessing depot performance!

Shortly after, the Neath superintendent changed the rules arbitrarily and no longer was there a league in which depots vied for position. The figures of locomotive availability continued to be published each month, but the league was transformed into a table with the position of each depot fixed in alphabetical order. Where did that place Swansea Paxton Street? At the bottom, below Swansea East Dock. . . .

★ ★ ★

On October 26th 1952, Her Majesty and Prince Philip travelled by Royal Train, via Shrewsbury and Craven Arms, to Llandrindod Wells, from whence they proceeded by road to inaugurate a new reservoir at Claerwen, a few miles west of Rhayader. (A plaque set in the platform now commemorates the spot where the Queen first set foot on Welsh soil after her accession to the throne.)

From Shrewsbury a G.W. "Castle" hauled the train to Llandrindod but limited clearance prohibited its use beyond that place.

After performing the opening ceremony at Claerwen, the Royal party rejoined the train at Llandovery, which then ran via the Llandilo–Carmarthen line to Milford Haven where the Royal Yacht lay at anchor, ready to begin a cruise into Scottish waters.

Three L.M.S. 2–8–0 8F locomotives were selected to work the Royal Train and all went to Crewe Works to be fitted with carriage warming apparatus. 48309, 48330 and 48707 were the locomotives chosen for this honour, but at that time only 48330 was allocated to Paxton Street. The other two were Salop (84G) engines, and they were all picked as being the three Stanier 8Fs with the lowest mileage since overhaul in Main Works. These were the only locos of that type I ever saw equipped with carriage warming apparatus, and I am not aware of any other L.M.S. freight locomotive type ever being selected to haul the Royal Train over such a distance.

Three locomotives were required since one would haul the empty stock from Builth Road to Llandindrod Wells, the second would work the train forward to Milford Haven, whilst the third would be a standby.

Preparation of an engine to work the Royal Train demanded a great deal of work, since first one would wish to eradicate any possibility of failure, and secondly to produce an engine which looked good. Since freight locomotives are not given the sort of paint finish accorded to passenger types, the latter requirement could only be arrived at by a great deal of hard work with file, emery cloth and elbow grease. My contacts with the stores liason inspectors at Crewe proved invaluable, and through their good offices I obtained a complete set of specially polished buffers, draw bars and screw couplings, front cylinder and steam chest cover plates for 48309, the engine I selected to work from Llandovery to Milford Haven.

The Neath mechanical inspector offered to relieve our burden by taking the standby, 48707, to an ex–G.W.depot for preparation. A few days later, because he was not satisfied with the job being done by that depot, he asked if I would agree to have 48707 back at Paxton Street for completion. In replacement he would take another Paxton Street engine for repair. A Super D, No.49148, was undergoing boiler washout and "X" scheme that day, after which it would require attention to a hot axlebox. He agreed to accept the loco at Danygraig shed, where the foreman was by now familiar with the peculiarities of L.M.S. horncheeks.

The necessary arrangements were made and early next morning

enginemen from Danygraig arrived to take 49148 to that depot for repairs. The Paxton Street running shift foreman on night duty met me when I arrived that morning, to say he had been in the shed yard as 49148 ran across the viaduct en route to Danygraig, and he'd never heard such a thunderous roar of steam and water from the chimney of a Super D in all his experience – and after that died away there had been a terrific clatter from the motion.

I rang the Danygraig leading fitter with this news, and asked him to have 49148 specially examined. Then I proceeded to busy myself with the Royal Train locos and forgot the incident.

The Royal Train journey was trouble free, and presumably to show appreciation of the effort put into preparation of 48309 and 48707 by everyone concerned, afterwards both engines were transferred to Paxton Street. We now had an additional three engines fitted with C.W.A for passenger train working during the steam heating season. The 2–8–0 8F could easily keep time with passenger trains over the Central Wales, and they were invaluable when eight special sleeping car trains were laid on to convey supporters of the Welsh rugby team from Swansea Victoria to Edinburgh during that winter.

A day or two after the Royal Train, I was dumbfounded by the unexpected arrival of the obviously irate Neath superintendent – a dyed–in–the–wool G.W.man – accompanied by his mechanical inspector. The former individual launched into a tirade concerning the condition of a locomotive I had sent to Danygraig for repair. The taper cotters in both crossheads were slack and they extended so far through the crossheads that at every piston stroke they had struck the axle of the leading coupled wheelset, causing damage which, in his opinion, would necessitate renewal of the axle.

In these comments one detected an oft–repeated derogatory theme concerning slack L.M.S. practices, but some moments passed before the realization dawned that he was talking about 49148 – the loco which had caused us such concern whilst in the hands of G.W.enginemen. Fortunately, the R.S.F. who had reported the incident was on duty and he confirmed my statement that the driver had mishandled the locomotive. After hearing I had asked the G.W. leading fitter at Danygraig to have the loco specially examined, the superintendent departed thence in his car, leaving behind an apologetic mechanical inspector.

Next day the D.M.P.S. returned, this time to convey me to Danygraig to inspect the damaged axle and comment thereon. There, I met the leading fitter, who admitted receiving my message and had intended to take the necessary action, but before he could do so a recurrent malaise forced him to go off duty, to be confronted on his return to work that very day by this situation. He had just emerged from a meeting with the D.M.P.S. and he had my heartfelt sympathy!

One is not aware of the action taken against the driver concerned, but this incident illustrates how easily trouble could be brought about by a poorly designed regulator valve, which in the hands of inexperienced drivers often caused water to be lifted up the main steam pipe into cylinders of Super Ds, where serious damage could be inflicted.

In the case of 49148, water coming into the front end of both cylinders had driven the piston rod cones into the mating cones in the crossheads, fracturing them both at the cotter slots and allowing the cotters to extrude and foul the axle. Without deliberate intent, it is certain no novice driver could cause this sort of damage by misuse of the regulator on most other types of locomotive.

Promotional prospects on the Western Region were somewhat restricted by the G.W. preference for footplate grades in the posts of shedmaster, and there was good reason to believe A.S.L.E.F. would devote its considerable influence to perpetuate this system, at least on Western Region. But at this period, salaried staff could only move from Region to Region in what was then known as Special Class grades A, B or C. Since I was two steps below "Special A" there appeared small prospect of getting back on L.M. Region without first making another promotional step on the Western.

Nevertheless, when a Chief Mechanical Foreman's post in the Special Class grade at Newton Heath (Manchester) appeared on the inter–Regional vacancy list in 1955, I submitted an application and was extremely surprised to receive an invitation to attend the interview.

This was held at Hunts Bank, the H.Q. offices of the L.M. Region's Central Division in Manchester. The panel consisted of the Divisional Motive Power Officer, the Newton Heath District Motive Power superintendent and the Divisional Locomotive Maintenance assistant.

Since none of the questions had floored me, I believed this (my first interview) had provided excellent experience in a new field and I returned to Swansea expecting nothing more. Two months passed and the hope of getting this job had totally vanished, when I received confirmation of my appointment of Newton Heath. I was instructed to report to the Hunts Bank office of the Divisional Motive Power Officer on the following Monday.

The Divisional Officer explained the delay had been due to the difficulty in getting H.Q. approval – apparently, not only had I been the junior person at the interview, but also a full grade beneath the others. I soon realised he had a specific reason for wishing to speak to me privately before I went on to Newton Heath shed: presumably drawing on his experience at District level, he stated that many chief mechanical foremen were too ready during normal working hours to attend derailments with the breakdown train, supervising the re–railing of wagons in sidings, which was often no more than labouring work and could be managed equally well by assistant foremen. As a result of this, overall supervison of the vital locomotive maintenance at the concentration depot often suffered.

CHAPTER IX
Steam finale

In 1955 the locomotive allocation at Newton Heath was as follows :

		Original Coy.	Build Date	Driving Wheels	Designer	No.
0-6-0ST	2F	L. & Y.	1891	4′6″	Aspinall	13
0-6-0	3F	L. & Y.	1889	5′1″	Aspinall	13
0-6-0	3F	L. & Y.	1909	5′1″	Aspinall	11
0-8-0	7F	L.M.S.	1926	4′8½″	Fowler	16
0-6-0T	3F	L.M.S.	1924	4′7″	Fowler	4
0-6-0	4F	L.M.S.	1924	5′3″	Fowler	3
2-6-0	2F	L.M.S.	1946	5′0″	Ivatt	2
2-6-2T	3P	L.M.S.	1930	5′3″	Fowler	5
2-6-4T	4P	L.M.S.	1935	5′9″	Stanier	14
2-6-4T	4P	L.M.S.	1945	5′9″	Fairburn	13
2-6-0	5F	L.M.S.	1926	5′6″	Hughes	25
4-6-0	5	L.M.S.	1934	6′0″	Stanier	37
4-6-0	6P	L.M.S.	1934	6′9″	Stanier	9
2-8-0	8F	L.M.S.	1935	4′8½″	Stanier	17
2-8-0	8F	Austerity	1941	4′8½″	Riddles	8
					Total	190

The fitting staff consisted of the following grades:

Foreman	Boilersmith	1	Apprentice Fitters	8
	Boilersmiths	8	Turners	3
Apprentice	Boilersmith	1	Coppersmiths	3
	Tubers	4	Apprentice Coppersmith	1
	Brickarch men	2	Fitters' mates	46
	Boilersmith mates	4	Carpenter	1
Assistant	Mechanical Foremen	2	Blacksmith	1
Leading	Fitters	3	Blacksmith's Striker	1
	Fitters	60	Shop Officemen	2
	Grade 3 Fitters	5		
			Total	156

Something in the order of 325 locomotives were allocated to sheds in the Newton Heath District, all of which came to us for valve and piston examination, plus hot axles. The depot had 24 pit roads under its roof, mechanical coaling and ash loading plants, a water treatment plant and two turntables, whilst there were three separate access routes between main lines and shed.

The shed was situated in the vee formed by Thorps Bridge Junction, some four miles north of Manchester Victoria station at a point where the Oldham line branched off the ex–L.& Y. main line to Yorkshire. Dean Lane station, on the Oldham line, is very close to the shed boundary and at that time there was a connection on the shed from the down line, controlled by Dean Lane box. On the opposite boundary of the shed yard there was another station, Newton Heath, on the main Yorkshire line. There was also a second connection on to the shed from this line, controlled by Newton Heath signalbox. The third, and most frequently used connection to the shed, was from Thorps Bridge Junction signal box.

A complex of buildings ran along the west side of the main line to Yorkshire for several hundred yards and, prior to amalgamation, this had been the main L. & Y. Carriage and Wagon Works. The southern–most buildings had been converted into a factory which produced pre–cast concrete components for the Chief Civil Engineer's department, but at the northern end the buildings were still used to store coaching stock and this was known as Lightbown Carriage Sidings.

The 24 pit roads of the depot were under one roof, but divided by a wall between roads 4 and 5 into two distinct sheds. The roof covering roads numbered 1 to 4 was high pitched and without the usual smoke troughing to protect its timbers from chimney sparks; this gave the place a very light and airy appearance, making it an ideal workshop for heavy repairs. This was where all valve and piston examinations and other heavy repairs were carried out. The main stores, machine shop, coppersmiths' shop, smithy and office block abutted the east wall, whilst tool cupboards and workbenches were arrayed along the opposite wall.

This part was so unlike the usual run of motive power depots everybody called it the "Parlour". Even the Chief Motive Power Superintendent's office referred to the place in this way in letters about its future use for diesels, and it survives today as part of the vast d.m.u. and diesel loco depot at Newton Heath. The wheel drop table and weighing machine tables have been removed, but all else remains virtually as the L.& Y. built it.

I believe Newton Heath was the only L.M.S. depot with a weighing machine capable of taking a ten–wheel locomotive, but its accuracy became rather suspect when one discovered that, if after weighing a locomotive it was then run up the shed yard and re–weighed, a quite different set of figures was obtained! The firm responsible for its maintenance was called in and spent several weeks overhauling the equipment but, although this work made some improvement, one could never expect the appliance to give more than a general trend in the distribution of axle loadings.

After a short period in digs close to the shed, I was able to obtain a house in a southern suburb of Manchester, about ten miles from Newton Heath. An important part of my duty was to take charge of the steam crane and breakdown train, and I was paid a percentage allowance to be "on call" after working hours. I told the D.M.P.S. I would install a telephone (at my own expense) and purchase a motor cycle to ensure my prompt arrival for derailments, but he agreed to this move with great reluctance.

Newton Heath breakdown train was called out to an average 260 derailments every year, and since many of these happened outside normal working hours, one could expect to be called out once or twice a week. But despite the distance I had to travel I was usually the first to arrive.

★ ★ ★

It was usual practice for the Chief Mechanical Foreman at a concentration depot to take personal control of staff engaged on valve and piston examinations and heavy repairs and when I took over, all ten fitters and mates employed on this work at Newton Heath were on regular daywork. My predecessor had believed he was able to exercise better control of these men and get more out of them on day work and to some extent I agreed with that opinion. It was foolish to force men to work shifts against their wishes, unless there was a compelling need for it – and that was not the case on "concentration" work. All the machinists and coppersmiths worked regular day turns, so that between 5/0pm and 8.0am work on locomotives was virtually confined to running repairs. After canvassing all the men concerned, I discovered that six fitters and mates were eager to work a full rota of shifts and the machinists and coppersmiths were prepared to work a night shift. The Shop Committee was consulted and agreement obtained to implement shift working – to such good effect that after a few weeks we had spare capacity to accept valve and piston examinations on locomotives from areas where fitters were scarce.

I was instructed to select a "Jubilee" to work the Royal Train from Aintree station where, after watching the Grand National, the Queen and Prince Philip would join the train for a journey over the Peak Forest route and via the Midland main line to Bedford. There the Royal couple were to spend a few days at a nearby stately home.

45691 *Prince Rupert* was chosen, and berthed in the Parlour for several days whilst we stripped her down for examination and overhaul. I made a point of emptying the tender tank for clean out, plus renewal of the water sieves. I was not happy about the paintwork and when I mentioned this to the D.M.P.S. he agreed with me. He had been trained in Horwich Works and must still have had a good relationship with the management there for two days later the paint shop foreman and several painters arrived from Horwich to repaint the Jubilee.

Newton Heath kept its own set of specially polished buffers, drawbar hooks and screw couplings in the smithy for Royal Train locos. When these were fitted, and 45691 stood in steam outside the shed on the morning of the Royal journey, she looked a real treat with brilliant sunshine glinting on the new paint and bright metal work.

The enginemen who were to run her light to Aintree climbed aboard and the firemen operated the live steam injector to fill the boiler; disaster struck when he shut it off and the injector clack stuck open! There was nothing to be done other than to drop the fire and blow all the steam out of the boiler in order to remove the offending injector clack valve and cage, which was mounted on top of the boiler. When removed, a small piece of grit was found trapped between valve and seating. Everyone present blamed the tender tank cleaning process I'd insisted on, claiming it would have been better to let sleeping dogs lie. . . . Grime and dust had settled all over *Prince Rupert* and it took a veritable army of cleaners to restore her former pristine condition. Fortunately, the rest of the journey was trouble free!

I selected two Black Fives to work our next Royal Train, which ran without any mechanical trouble – but there was trouble of a different nature. Her Majesty was visiting several towns in the north, the first of which was to be Guide Bridge. The D.M.P.S. invited me to accompany him to watch the arrival of the Royal Train at that station, which was in the territory of the Longsight D.M.P.S., John Knapman, who was also of course in attendance there.

The usual red carpet had been rolled out over which the Queen would walk to the station exit. We waited near the platform end, where also stood the mandatory "flagman". His position had been carefully measured, and it was intended the driver of the first Black Five should bring the train to a halt when its cab drew level with the red flag, and the

Queen would alight on the red carpet. . . .

Imagine our dismay when the train entered the station and the first engine ran past the red flag held out by the astonished flagman. The driver of the second engine stopped *his* cab opposite the flag and Her Majesty had to walk back a full engine's length to reach the carpet. . . .

After a short visit to Guide Bridge, the Royal Train left for Wigan Wallgate, hauled by the same engines but crewed by fresh enginemen. I was not present to witness this second minor disaster, but again the train overshot its mark – this time by an even greater margin! The position of the flagman was blamed on this occasion: he had been positioned on Wallgate's island platform, therefore his red flag signal was on the fireman's side and, since the platform has a severe left–hand curvature, by the time the fireman spotted him and shouted "Whoa!" both engines had run past. . . . We will draw a veil over the interview the D.M.P.S. had with these drivers next day.

Despite a much larger allocation of engines it was noticeable that the wheel drop was used less frequently for hot axles at Newton Heath than Paxton Street: at the former we seemed to use the wheel drop mainly to change tender wheels for loose tyres.

Stanier had introduced a method of securing tyres on wheel centres by the usual shrinkage fit, but with matching radial grooves in wheel centre and tyre, into which a Gibson ring was fitted; a lip on the inside of the tyre then secured this assemblage in position.

Special tyre thickness measuring gauges were provided at depots and tyre thicknesses were recorded on the appropriate document for each locomotive. Tyres were approximately 3″ thick when new, but they wore in service and were machined back to correct profile during overhaul in Main Works. A minimum tyre thickness was laid down and as this was approached, tender wheel tyres of the Gibson–ring variety were particularly prone to work loose. This was not a dangerous condition since the ring prevented the tyre working off the wheel centre, but a loose tyre could move in a radial direction relative to its original position on the wheel centre.

In my experience, coupled wheel tyres of comparable thickness never moved on wheel centres and one can only attribute this to the greater mass of the wheel centres which permitted better dissipation of heat generated during braking.

As soon as an examining fitter reported a loose tyre, the foreman would inspect it personally and order a replacement pair of wheels, quoting the tender number and the tyre thickness. If, in his opinion the tyre was safe, the locomotive would be listed to work local freights only, and a daily check of the tyre would be made until the replacement wheels arrived, or it became necessary to take the loco out of traffic.

In 1956 an afternoon passenger train from Manchester to Leeds was derailed at a junction outside Droylsden, on the ex–L.N.W. main line between those cities. The train consisted of seven coaches, hauled by a Newton Heath Black Five, No.45223. The whole train, including the engine and tender, was completely derailed but all stayed upright and no one was injured.

When our breakdown train arrived at the site, I was met by the assistant Divisional Operating Superintendent who told me he was certain that the tender of 45223 had been the first to become derailed, immediately prior to negotiating the junction south of the station. Gorton steam crane and breakdown brain had been called out to assist us, and they re–railed 45223 while we took charge of the derailed coaches. It was a straight–forward job, but both myself and the assistant Divisional Motive Power Superintendent (who had accompanied our breakdown train) were very concerned by the suggestion that the tender might be responsible for the accident. Examination of it revealed no apparent defect, but as soon as the breakdown train arrived back on Newton Heath shed in the early hours of the morning, we spent a couple of hours going through the records of 45223. The locomotive had a fairly high mileage since shops and was due for shopping proposal the following month. There had been a couple of drivers' reports of rough riding, but that was normal for engines of this mileage. But we discovered that since the previous overhaul in Crewe Works, at different times all the tender wheelsets had been renewed because of loose tyres.

A Ministry of Transport inquiry would be held into this accident, but in the meantime B.R.officers would be anxious to establish the cause. Accordingly 45223 was taken into Horwich Works for examination, where it was discovered that the weight of the tender was unevenly distributed on the wheels.

The tender had been derailed to the right of the tracks, and the righthand leading wheel carried considerably less weight than the lefthand wheel. The weight distribution was fairly even on the middle wheels, but it was reversed over the trailing pair, with the right one carrying more weight than the left. In other words, there was a diagonal difference in weight distribution.

We were asked to weigh a selection of these 4,000 gallon tenders at Newton Heath and we found the same diagonal wheel loading variation on most tenders, which seemed to indicate that whilst this might have been a contributory factor , it certainly was not the cause.

In fact the M.O.T. inquiry blamed a permanent way defect for the derailment, but long before that was held the C.M.E.E. of London Midland Region had taken steps to remedy another defect which came to light during examination of 45223 in Horwich Works.

When depots ordered replacement tender wheelsets the only dimension called for on the requisition was a tyre thickness. When a tyre became loose there was a tendency for wear to occur at the contact area on the wheel centre and, after the loose tyre was removed, this surface would be turned in the lathe, thus reducing the diameter. As a result, when a depot ordered a wheelset with 2½″ tyre thickness, there was no guarantee the new wheels would be the same overall diameter as those which had been removed.

Each tender wheelset from 45223 varied in diameter by as much as ⅜″, and to eradicate the possibility of this happening in future, every time metal was turned off the diameter of tender wheel centres, a letter was stamped thereon to indicate the new diameter, which was quoted with the tyre thickness when depots requisitioned a pair of replacedment tender wheels.

The Modernisation plan for British Railways included renewal of many bridges, and breakdown steam cranes were much in demand to dismantle the existing metal girders and lift the pre–stressed concrete girders in place.

This work often took a complete weekend, and we would leave the depot on Saturday afternoon, not returning until Monday morning. The weight and length of the concrete units frequently required two steam cranes to lift them in position, standing on either side of the bridge. We worked with steam cranes from Wakefield, Leeds, Bank Hall, Edge Hill, Gorton, Crewe and Chester, and it was bonanza time for everyone, except me. I was paid by a ridiculous system relating to the amount of Sunday duty one had performed during the previous two years. It could rise to 25 per cent of one's salary, but my predecessor had been a sick man which restricted this bonus to 5 per cent when I took over. My salary was £800 p.a., which meant I received £40 p.a. for all this Sunday duty!

During this period a serious accident occurred at Chapel–en–le–Frith, on the ex–L.N.W. line between Buxton and Manchester. A freight left Buxton headed by a Stanier 2–8–0. When the driver made a brake application, the steam brake pipe on the footplate fractured and power to the locomotive brakes was lost. The train picked up speed and the fireman leapt off the footplate, but the driver stayed at his post and was killed when the runaway hurtled into the rear of a stationary goods train in Chapel station. The guard of that train was also killed, a signalbox demolished and a d.m.u. in the down platform was also damaged. The driver was posthumously awarded the George Cross for his bravery in staying on the 8F in a vain attempt to bring the train to a halt.

Crewe and Derby breakdown trains went to the site on Saturday, but early on Sunday morning Newton Heath was sent to take over from the Crewe breakdown train and for the following six weeks, every Sunday at 6.0a.m, I waited on Stockport station to join Newton Heath breakdown crew en route to Chapel for a 12–hour day of loading damaged wagons.

Diesel multiple units were already operating passenger services between Bury and Manchester, but maintenance was carried out in Bury electric train depot,and the Motive Power department had nothing to do with these, apart from supplying drivers from Bury loco shed to operate them. However, when two young engineers were appointed to the posts of diesel assistant and diesel inspector at Hunt's Bank Divisional office, one realised it would not be very long before Newton Heath got its quota of "Spam Cans".

Horace Smith, the Divisional Mechanical Inspector for steam locomotives, was infuriated by the Management Staff grade awarded to John Fore, the new Diesel Inspector, pointing out that on the Central Division there were well over a thousand steam locos and as yet, no diesels!

My relationship with Horace Smith was excellent and we saw a lot of him at Newton Heath, usually investigating some design problem in company with his opposite number, Ray Morgan, from Horwich Works. I had a contact in Divisional Office who warned me of Horace Smith's forthcoming Standard Practices Investigation at Newton Heath, in time for me to go through all my locomotive records. What I saw satisfied me the investigation would reveal an improvement over the one he had carried out prior to my appointment, and in fact this proved to be so.

Patricroft, the large ex–L.N.W. shed serving Manchester (Exchange), had recently been transferred from the Springs Branch (Wigan) Motive Power District to us at Newton Heath and this also meant a transfer from the Western Division Crewe H.Q. to the Central Divisional Manchester H.Q. Reg Smith, Divisional Mechanical Inspector at Crewe, had recently completed a Standard Practices Investigation at Patricroft and he visited Newton Heath to present his report. We had a good old chin wag about our time together at Swansea and Salop, and I learned Reg was retiring in a few months time and going to live in Tarporley with his daughter.

A few months before we received our first allocation of d.m.u.s I went on several visits to factories concerned with supplying engines and transmissions for these vehicles: A.E.C. factory in Southall, Self–Change Gears in Coventry, Leyland at Chorley, a Lucas works in London, plus a six–week course at the B.R. College of Transport in Derby.

The first d.m.u. scheme was one of sixteen twin power car sets for the Manchester Victoria to Oldham and Rochdale trains, and before the implementation of these services, in order to have the use of the "Parlour" for maintaining the d.m.u. sets, it was necessary to transfer all Newton Heath District valve and piston examination work to Patricroft. It was also necessary to supplement the fitting staff there by four fitters and mates from Newton Heath, but the supervision at Patricroft was not adequate to allow this work to be carried out on a shift basis.

The numbers of d.m.u.s increased as successive schemes were introduced. The Bury – Manchester sets were transferred to us and much of my time and energy was being devoted to supervising the maintenance of d.m.u.s. – to such an extent I was failing in my duty to exercise supervision over what was happening on the other side of the wall, in the steam shed. Of course, steam locomotive allocation was now falling with the introduction of d.m.u.s. and diesel locomotives, but I had to thank my assistant foremen for continuing to maintain our steam engines to a high standard.

Newton Heath was never what might be termed a main line passenger shed: witness to this fact only eight or nine Jubilees were allocated, and only four of these worked long–distance passenger trains each day between Manchester Victoria and Glasgow Central. We had but two trains to London, consisting of vacuum–braked goods vehicles hauled by our Black Fives between Moston Sidings and Camden, and Brewery Sidings and Willesden. As the largest shed on the ex–L.&Y (and rated by many as the largest on the L.M.S.), Newton Heath locomotives were largely confined within the territorial boundaries of that railway, which was not the Central Division of the L.M.Region. As a result of this, when main line diesel locomotives began to appear on the scene, none was allocated to work at Newton Heath.

Work began on demolishing part of the steam shed roof west of the parlour to make way for a new four–track depot for diesel multiple units, together with new fuel oil tanks and re–fueling facilities. Prior to this we had refuelled from two ancient rail tanks which caused us no end of trouble.

* * *

Since the introduction of the first d.m.u. service in 1958, I had spent several hours each Sunday at the depot on an entirely voluntary basis, and one morning the running shift foreman asked me if I would instruct a driver in the operation of d.m.u.controls whilst he drove a spare two–car set to Victoria to replace a set which had failed. Since there was no d.m.u.–trained driver available, I agreed, but made the serious error of taking the controls personally, whilst the driver advised me of the signals, speeds and crossings en route. We then returned to Newton Heath with the defective d.m.u. in like manner.

On the Monday morning the D.M.P.S. sent for me. An angry deputation of footplate staff had just left his office after complaining bitterly about my action, which they quite rightly claimed could have been avoided had management provided enough trained drivers to cover these emergencies. The D.M.P.S. was surprised to learn it was my habit to spend a few hours each Sunday at the depot and, after he had pointed out the error of my ways in having taken the controls personally and prohibited any future action of that nature, I believed that was the end of the affair. I heard the matter had been reported to the A.S.L.E.F. London H.Q., who had passed it on to the L.M.R. H.Q. at Euston, and realised the D.M.P.S. would be required to answer some awkward questions, but to this day I cannot understand why it was considered necessary to send the Divisional Diesel Inspector to pass me out to move diesel multiple units and diesel shunting locomotives.

* * *

With the introduction of diesel traction, managerial work load had increased enormously and by 1960 it was deemed necessary to have a Locomotive Shedmaster at Newton Heath and I was appointed to the position. Fortunately, I was already familar with most aspects of my new duties, since I had always acted as *locum* for the assistant D.M.P.S., and for the shedmasters at Swansea and Upper Bank.

In my new post, I would now be paid for the actual hours worked on such duty at overtime rates, which is illustrative of the complexities and injustices of a salary structure carried over from the Victorian era.

I was appointed at the commencement of the summer season, at a time when railways were still providing scores of excursion trains each weekend to convey holidaymakers to their destinations. As the traditional Lancashire Wakes Weeks approached we were supplied with schedules covering the extra trains needed for each town, and the types of locomotive required to haul them. The responsibility for providing these additional locomotives had previously been accepted by the office of the Divisional Motive Power Superintendent at Hunts

Bank, but this year they had indicated their inability to perform this function, and to all of us at Newton Heath this seemed a total abrogation of Divisonal responsibility.

The Lancashire Wakes Weeks began with Oldham and the surrounding towns of Royton, Middleton, Shaw, etc. and it was also the heaviest in terms of additional locomotives required. The special train services began on the Friday night, when some dozen or so overnight trains were routed to resorts on the south coast. On the Saturday we had to provide over forty extra locomotives for trains destined for towns on the east and west coasts, also to those along the North Wales coast.

On the previous Monday I began to withdraw all the visiting 4–6–0 and 2–6–0 class 5 locomotives from foreign depots which came to Newton Heath on freight services and, with the help of Power Control at Hunts Bank, they were replaced by locomotives unsuitable for passenger work. These foreign locomotives were then recorded in our official records as being under repairs for a variety of fictitious reasons, and by the Friday morning we had collected a score or more. Garage depots in the district sent us their spare engines and all boiler washing plus "X" scheme work at Newton Heath on the Friday and Saturday was cancelled. It was necessary to stop fourteen engines every week day and seven on Saturday morning if we were to keep locomotives within the twelve to sixteen day period allowed between boiler washout and "X" Scheme, and this cancellation would provide a few additional locos. In an effort to recover some of the leeway this caused to the depot's boiler washing programme, the boilerwashers and extra fitting staff were brought on duty on Sunday.

This was the plan adopted, to a degree dependent on the Operating Superintendent's requirements, for the Wakes week of each town, but one began to doubt if the enormous, but hidden, cost was worth while, for news of near–empty trains began to filter back to us from our drivers.

At the time when d.m.u.s. were introduced, we at depots had been enthused by reports of a 100 per cent increase in passenger loadings on those services, only to be deflated by the revelation this resulted merely from a doubling of single figures . . . .

Now it began to seem the effort depot staff put in to providing locos for these extra holiday trains was even less financially rewarding for British Railways.

Towards the middle of 1961 London Midland Region began a reorganisation of its Divisional and District levels of management, which would affect all departments. Engineering maintenance was divided into five separate departments: Outdoor Machinery, Road

Motor, Electric Traction (where application), Motive Power, and Carriage & Wagon, but these would in future be combined in a new organisation under one Divisional Maintenance Engineer. The Manchester Division would comprise the former Longsight and Newton Heath Districts, and the same re–structuring arrangements applied to the Operating and Commercial departments.

As an interim measure of supervision, until the new Divisional organisations settled down, the old Central, Midland and Western Divisional authorities would continue, but in a new guise under the titles North West Line, Midland Line and Western Line, each with its Line Manager and Line Maintenance Engineer . . . . a rose by any other name, one might think.

The North West Line H.Q. would continue to be in Manchester, but since the former L.&Y. Offices at Hunts bank were needed for the new Divisional set–up, three floors of Sunlight House office block in Manchester were leased to house the new Line organisation. Hunts Bank, which once housed the entire management organisation of the Lancashire & Yorkshire, was now able to house only the H.Q. organisation of one Division of British Railways!

In March 1962 I applied for the post of Headquarters Diesel Inspector in the North West Line organisation, and was appointed by the Line Maintenance Foreman at Newton Heath seven years earlier.

Henceforth, my duties were entirely divorced from the rapidly diminishing stock of steam engines and concentrated upon the small but expanding fleet of main line diesel locos. At that time those were allocated to individual depots, where examinations were performed alongside steam engines, amidst the smoke and dust and rapidly deteriorating conditions in steam sheds.

Everybody involved with the maintenance of diesel traction in those early days deplored the decision to maintain them in steam sheds, in conditions that adversely affected electrical equipment, and many engine components. We all believed their introduction should have been delayed until the planned new depots were ready. From the writings widely available in book form nowadays, penned by individuals then at top levels of management, one learns this was a universally held opinion among the senior engineers at executive level. The conclusion that this untimely and precipitate introduction of diesel traction was forced upon them from an even higher level is inevitable.

The boundaries of the Western and Northwestern Lines were re–drawn to include everything north of Crewe in the Manchester–based Line Manager's territory, which was fortunate since prior to that decision all we had were a few dozen diesel shunting locos, and a fleet of d.m.u.s. Henceforth the Northwest Line D.M.E. would be responsible for some thirty class 40 locos based at Longsight, Edge Hill and Carlisle Upperby. A few Sulzer class 25 locos were allocated to Trafford Park and Longsight and later the entire fleet of twenty Metro–Vick Co–Bo locos (powered by the Crossley two–stroke engines) were transferred to Barrow–in–Furness.

It was part of my duty to supervise the preparation of diesel locos for the Royal Train and to accompany the loco on its journey in case of technical difficulty. The reliable E.E.Type 4s (class 40) always worked these trains on the West Coast main line, singly or in multiple, and I made several uneventful journeys aboard them between England and Scotland.

It had long been L.M.S. practise to exclude Footplate Inspectors from the footplates of steam engines working "Grove" or "Deepdene" trains. These code names respectively described a full Royal Train, and a regular passenger train which conveyed a royal party in several coaches from the Royal Train ("The Royal Highlander" between Euston and Inverness for example occasionally being used for the latter purpose). The reason for the exclusion of Footplate Inspectors was said to have been a delay en route, caused by an altercation between driver and inspector, but whatever the cause, I understand the L.M.S. was unique in this among the railways of Britain. The Chief Footplate Inspector always accompanied the enginemen on the train which preceded the Royal, and they had come to accept the situation without murmur, until technical men began to accompany diesel locos. Of course, my job was not concerned with time–keeping or the handling of the train, but to be on hand in case of technical trouble. Nevertheless, it was a sore point among the fraternity of Footplate Inspectors! Years later, when the responsibility for Footplate Inspectors and enginemen was transferred to the Operating department, their voices were successfully raised in protest and they nowadays ride with Royal Train locomotives on the L.M.R., but are still accompanied by a technician, albeit of rather lower status.

In 1964 a new L.M.R. Inspectorate was set up under the aegis of A.E.Robson, C.M.E.E. (L.M.R.). British Rail C.M.E.E.(HQ) issued detailed maintenance requirements for all forms of traction and rolling stock and the purpose of this organisation was to investigate the efficiency of depots and main works in performing this task. Inspectorates were set up at the main works of Crewe, Derby, Horwich and Wolverton, also at the Line offices in Manchester, Derby and Crewe. I was appointed to the new Inspectorate in Manchester, and for the next two years we beavered away happily until a new C.M.E.E. at Derby decided the inspectorate was not a good idea and made us all redundant. . . .

I then joined the Preston Divisional Maintenance Engineer's organisation and spent much of my time at Kingmoor and Upperby depots in Carlisle. The railways began to shrink with alarming rapidity, wagon–load freight traffic vanished so quickly that the giant new marshalling yard at Kingmoor, only completed a year or two earlier, soon became the biggest white elephant in the history of the West Coast Main Line. A smart two–road depot for the maintenance of shunting locomotives had been built at the southern extremity of the yard, with its associated diesel fuel tanks and re–fuelling equipment, and a little further south a new main line diesel depot was in the process of building.

In 1967, the former Carriage & Wagon Engineer of the Barrow Division, Bert Robertson, and myself were asked to investigate the riding qualities and general condition of coaching stock on all the new 100m.p.h. electric train services.

The Derby Research section had produced an electronic instrument, which when placed on the floor of a coach, registered the vertical and lateral oscillation on a meter. An engineer had published a paper concerning the riding characteristics of passenger–carrying railway vehicles, in which he had allotted a numerical value to the various degrees of ride comfort – or discomfort. These numbers were reproduced on the meter, and thus armed Bert Robertson and I sallied forth. He was a great companion – a Scot from Aberdeen with a craggy sort of face, a fund of risque jokes and a tendency to become unintelligible if he allowed his Scots accent to get out of control when he became excited.

We checked and reported on the ride values obtained in each vehicle and inspected and reported on all defects. Since most of these were found in the toilets of vehicles, and copies of these reports were sent to the Carriage & Wagon Depots responsible for maintenance, it was inevitable we should become entitled "Lavatory Engineers". . . .

Nevertheless, it was good experience for the job in the C & W section of the L.M.R. C.M.E.E. at Derby I was to hold for the next ten years. It was a post which kept me constantly on the move throughout the length and breadth of the L.M.R., and often on other Regions as well until my retirement in 1979.